Hans-Jost Frey

Interruptions

translated and with an introduction by
Georgia Albert

STATE UNIVERSITY OF NEW YORK PRESS

Originally published in 1989 by Edition Howeg, Zurich, under the title *Unterbrechungen.*

Published by
State University of New York Press

© 1996 State University of New York

For information, address the State University of New York Press,
State University Plaza, Albany, NY 12246

Production by Bernadine Dawes • Marketing by Fran Keneston

Library of Congress Cataloging-in-Publication Data

Frey, Hans-Jost, 1933–
        Interruptions / Hans-Jost Frey : translated by Georgia Albert.
            p.   cm. — (SUNY series, Intersections—philosophy and critical
theory)
        ISBN 0-7914-3019-7. —ISBN 0-7914-3020-0 (pbk.)
        1. Criticism. I. Title. II. Series: Intersections (Albany, NY)
PN81.F686 1996   96-1940

1 2 3 4 5 6 7 8 9

CONTENTS

FRAGMENTARY STATES

Writing Fragmentarily

Interruptions is Hans-Jost Frey's third major publication, preceded by the long essay "Verszerfall" (collected in Frey and Lorenz, *Kritik des freien Verses* [1980]) and by the volume of readings of poetry *Studien über das Reden der Dichter* (1986).[1] It represents one aspect of a larger project, other parts of which have since appeared in *Der unendliche Text* (1990) and in still uncollected essays. The consistent concern of this project, for which *Interruptions* lays the theoretical ground, is a deceptively basic question: whether it is possible to define— i.e., to delimit—what constitutes a text for the purposes of literary study. At issue is not the decision about which texts are worthy of being read by virtue of their literary or other qualities, but a more fundamental, and prior, determination, namely where and how a text— any text—begins and ends: what happens at the border that marks each text off from all others, from the blank page and from an "outside" however defined. In his recent work, Frey insistently returns to the liminal zone that, surrounding texts, indicates the separation and transition between meaninglessness and meaning, and asks what consequences might be produced for the institution of literary studies by a mode of reading that would not presume to know a priori where a text's border is traced and what happens in the crossing.

In *Der unendliche Text* Frey's project takes the form of an inquiry into the problem posed for literary hermeneutics by the essentially

---

[1] *Studies in Poetic Discourse: Mallarmé, Baudelaire, Rimbaud, Hölderlin,* trans. William Whobrey (Stanford, Calif.: Stanford University Press, 1995).

intertextual nature of all texts. If translation, revision, quotation, and so on—all possible relations between texts—are not simply accidents that come to the text from the outside but are constitutive of it, then a text is never actually finished or complete, since its contact with other texts will necessarily continue to open it up to new possibilities of meaning. The first casualty of such a conception of the text, Frey argues, is literary history as a linear chronology, which depends for its coherence on its treating texts as complete, closed-off units belonging to a past that can be filed away. For if texts are read in their ever-renewed contexts, they are never a part of "literary history" as a sequence of authors and works but transform themselves according to specifically *textual* paradigms, acquiring a history of their own—one not congruent either with the biography of their authors or with the social and intellectual history of their readers. More recently, in readings of Coleridge's marginalia and Hölderlin's manuscripts, Frey has recast the question in terms not of the chronological, but of the physical borders and margins of texts.[2] In all these cases the analysis shows that the text's contact with the outside—the permeability of its border—opens it up to possibilities of interpretation that are excluded from the start by the presupposition, central not only to literary history but also to the institution of national literature departments as well as to the current debate about canon formation, that texts have identifiable historical and geographical limits.

To say that *Interruptions* lays the theoretical ground for this project is to assign it a position of great responsibility and import, a responsibility and import that the book seems at pains to shun. For *Interruptions* is not a book of literary criticism or theory in any traditional sense. Even the most hurried of browsers will notice at first glance the absence of quotations of any kind, the extreme sparseness of the

---

[2] "Überlegungen an der Textgrenze," *MLN* 109 (1994): 356–71; "Hölderlins Marginalisierung der Sprache," to appear in Aris Fioretos, ed., *The Solid Letter: New Readings of Friedrich Hölderlin,* forthcoming.

scholarly apparatus accompanying the text, and the unconventional typographical arrangement of several of the pieces. And indeed even a less cursory glance would seem to confirm that these texts might more fittingly have been published in a different form—as short stories, for example, or prose poems. This is especially true of the parables or allegories collected under the title "Stories" in the first section of the book, but it could be applied to the other texts as well—all "literary" without doubt by their intense and sustained preoccupation with their own mode of expression. In fact, the only portion of the book that can be identified as openly speaking about literature—and about literary studies—is the middle section, which, under the title "Break-off," itself represents a break from the rest of the volume, discussing in more traditionally metalinguistic terms the problem addressed in other ways in the first and last third of the book. Yet the parables of the first part and the descriptions of everyday situations (waiting, boredom, absentmindedness) of the third, while less explicitly *about* matters of literary relevance, are in fact as rigorously concerned with the question asked by the book as the more openly theoretical middle section, offering as it were a refracted image of it.

The recurrent and insistent object of reflection in these texts—one hesitates for obvious reasons to call it their unifying theme—is the problem of the fragment. The fundamental property of the fragment for Frey is the resistance it opposes to the ordering gesture of understanding. In the specifically linguistic case of the fragmentary text, this gesture is that of the critic who, wishing for clear-cut answers, catalogs the fragment either as accidental or as intentional and interprets it accordingly. But, Frey argues, by trying to *know* the fragment this decision precisely deprives itself of the object of its query, since the intentional fragment, which contains in itself the reason for its incompletion, is in fact a whole, and the accidental fragment is simply part of a larger whole. To force a fragment into either of these two categories is to ignore precisely what is essential to it: the undecidable question as to whether the actual occurrence of its breaking off, which "just happens—incomprehensibly" (p. 49), can be recuperated into a system of meaning. Being "neither a whole nor a part," the fragment "cannot be understood from the perspective of the whole" (p. 26), which means that it is not certain whether it can be understood at all. As Frey shows, this fundamental structure of the fragment as inexplicable interruption is not found exclusively in the domain of literature, but inhabits all realms of human experience, an undesirable guest wherever closure and definite answers are sought. In all its manifestations, the fragment poses a constant challenge to the usual oppositions of finiteness and infinity, part and whole, and refuses to be sacrificed to the need for an ordered structure in which to live and think, with its requirement that everything be assigned a position in a larger entity able to contain and justify it. This applies to the fragment in its narrower literary definition as well as to the "fragmentary states" described in the third section of the book: mental and existential attitudes (exhaustion, indifference, hopelessness, daredevilry . . .) that, by escaping closure, reflect the fragment's resistance to codification and ordering into a system.

In the opening text of "Fragmentary States," in keeping with an interest in the status of the law that punctuates the book, Frey interrogates the implications that the possibility of "living fragmentarily" (living without faith in the ability of death to produce the completion, and meaning, of one's life) has for morality and responsibility, and argues that "it is a great accomplishment of the law" (p. 56) to recognize that there are situations that escape the binary structure of right and wrong on which it is based. The only legal system that could responsibly face actual irresponsibility—the incapacity to answer for one's actions—is presumably the permanently unfinished one of the fictional community described in the parable "Law" (p. 12), a community that, taking seriously its recognition of the arbitrariness (i.e., the irresponsibility) of its laws, keeps them in perpetual flux, considering each crime a legitimate challenge to their validity and involving the criminal in the process of revision. "Of course," Frey argues in "Living Fragmentarily," "the claim to validity is necessary to the law. But to posit [setzen] a law [Gesetz] as definitive is usurpation. No human law—and we do not have another one—can overcome its status as linguistic position [Setzung] and the lack of a guarantee" (p. 56). The only law that can be upheld and enforced without recourse to an epistemological and ethical compromise is the one that is aware of its status as mere positing at all times. Thus the fictional narrator of "Law" is able to declare proudly: "[O]ur nation has no stability, but that we don't pretend it has any is its strength" (p. 13). A utopia of sorts, the state described in "Law" may also appear as an ideal version of the university as a community so committed to critical vigilance that it is permanently engaged in the revision of what constitutes it as a community.

In the section of the book devoted primarily to the fragment as a literary phenomenon, the counterpart to the law turns out to be *Literaturwissenschaft*—literary scholarship or criticism at its most policelike, the kind of encounter with texts that wishes to produce understanding as a means of control—and the fragment plays the role of the lawbreaker. The fragment is a problem for any system, for any thinking (Frey calls it "violent") that has closure as its goal. By resisting integration into any of the categories available to literary scholarship and refusing to be understood as either accident or intentional act, it poses a problem for any literary scholarship or hermeneutics invested in mastery, and forces it either to ignore the fragment, renouncing it as an object of study, or to question its own validity. But in Frey's argument the fragment, far from being an exception to the success of an otherwise acceptable method (the systematic explaining away of the text), is merely the place where the contradiction inherent in the method is most clearly visible, since the interest in explaining a text implies a belief that the text is "lacking" in some sense, that in order to *mean* it needs the supplement of a commentary or exegesis. Every text is, in this sense, a fragment, and causes the same difficulty that is posed by the fragment in the strict sense: if its "lack" is a fault, and something is "missing," the text is no longer "whole" and cannot be treated as such; if the "lack" is constitutive of it, the attempt to supply what is missing by an explanation is irrelevant and a violation precisely of what is essential to it, namely, its lack (p. 32). But moreover, the fragment brings into view an even more fundamental characteristic of linguistic constructs, namely, that they are always, no matter their degree of complexity, unable to account for their own borders—for their beginning and ending. The abrupt and always unprepared start of a text can be endowed with meaning only retrospectively, while its end, since it can only happen when it is no longer *said*, is always only an interruption (pp. 23–24). Thus, the central task of every text will be to endow with meaning the actual events of its beginning and ending, and that task will necessarily fail, leaving those moments as it were in excess. As a result, Frey argues, an approach to literature that conceives its aim as understanding without remainder must either ignore the challenge posed by the fragment or give up what is essential for its own project.

Analogously to the solution proposed in "Law" for the problem created by any rigorous questioning of the validity of the law, the solution suggested for literary studies is not to find other strategies for control, but to recognize that such control is a product of fear and can only be maintained by repressing what threatens it. A discourse able to act on this recognition and give up its "claim to power," Frey argues in a passage that echoes his critique of the law in "Living Fragmentarily," would be one in which any relation is "posited [*gesetzt*] only so that it can be deposed [*zersetzt*]" (p. 33). In other words, such a discourse would be engaged in the same process of self-revision exemplified by the legal system of the community described in "Law." Thus, the final passage in "Paradox" parallels the conclusion of "Law," stating: "Any discourse on the fragment that is not simply reductive becomes paradoxical. Seen from the perspective of a repressive literary scholarship, this is its 'weakness,' but thanks to this weakness it can come close to its object without having to coincide with it and break off" (p. 33).

What would such a discourse look like? Its master figure, Frey suggests, is the paradox, which affirms and disables the logic of its statement at the same time. And paradox is indeed at the heart of the effort of *Interruptions*: the paradox or, as Frey also says, the irony that "there is nothing to say" about the unjustifiable breaking off of the fragment, since "what breaks off justifiably has ended" (p. 72) and is therefore no longer fragment. To comment successfully on the fragment—to explain it—would be to take away what is most proper to it, namely, its fragmentariness. What is called for, then, is a different kind of commentary, one that no longer strives for explanation as a means of control and that counters at each step the tendency to systematicity: in short, one that distinguishes itself from *Literaturwissenschaft* by its indifference—in Frey's sense—to any "claim to power." And indeed *Interruptions* exhibits marks of that indifference on all levels. There is, first of all, the division of the book into three apparently incompatible sections: a collection of short fictional texts followed by a series of theoretical and philosophical essays and finally by the more descriptive texts of the third part. Frey himself provides a characterization of this way of proceeding in a recent essay on Walter Benjamin's technique of the treatise. It does not take much forcing to apply these lines to the project of *Interruptions* as well:

> In place of a seamless continuity of argument or a chain of evidence, there is a movement of thought that again and again is

interrupted and begins anew in order to approach the object again and again from different angles.[3]

This repeated approach "from different angles," this halting and hesitant attempt to treat the question from a new side each time, is also found on a more local level in some of the individual texts. It is no accident, for instance, that the text that opens the book (or perhaps already "interrupts" it, as its title suggests) is a dialogue, and a dialogue engaged in asking what a dialogue is:

- So why don't you let me finish talking?
○ Because we are in conversation and conversation is perhaps this: that one does not finish talking. . . . Conversation is interruption. (P. 6)

The dialogue or conversation, conceived here less as a process of completion of one speaker's thought by the other's words than as reciprocal interference (or, in Friedrich Schlegel's formulation, as a "chain of fragments"), could be seen as a figure for the organization of the book as a whole, with each of the parts intervening to interrupt the other parts' tentative answers and recast the question in a different way, "throwing constellations like dice" (p. 69) in the manner of the improviser.

Finally, another sign of the book's refusal to bow to the necessity of systematicity is its openness to what it calls "the unforeseen": a trait thematized in "Surprise" and in the text about the writer "on the side" and also discussed in the essay on Benjamin, where Frey calls it "a methodical surrender to chance." One of the forms taken by "chance" here is the accident of language, intervening for example

---

[3] "On Presentation in Benjamin," trans. Michael Shae, in *Walter Benjamin: Theoretical Questions,* edited by David S. Ferris (Stanford, Calif.: Stanford University Press, forthcoming).

in the coincidence that allows a simple capitalization to turn the words *ziellos, zwecklos, sinnlos* and *zeitlos*—adjectives respectively meaning aimless, purposeless, senseless and timeless—into compounds of the noun *Los*—the lot assigned by fate or a lottery ticket (p. 59). What is *sinnlos*, senseless, is always on the verge of becoming a *Sinn-los*, the number drawn in the lottery of sense, in which the attainment of meaning depends on chance. Similarly, the successfully achieved conclusion of a relationship is available to one of the characters of the story "End" (p. 19) only by way of a potentially infinite, and purely unmotivated, series of assonances: "Walls *[Wände]* full of volumes *[Bände]* of rhymes without end *[Ende]*"—a sentence where the potentially endless series of rhymes that structures its approach to its own ending, the word "end," is also named in it as the character's only way to achieve the end of the relationship, her ability to bring it to a conclusion by endowing it with meaning. So it is hardly a surprise when the series of rhymes is reopened immediately afterwards by the word *Händen*, hands: the phrase "man kann sie mit Händen greifen," an idiom roughly equivalent to "it's as plain as the nose on your face," at the same time names the drive to control the proliferation of signifiers (and signification) with the gesture of the hands grabbing and holding on to something (in "Paradox" Frey refers to the etymological connection between the verb *greifen* and *Begriff*, concept) and defeats it by marking the reopening of the series of signifiers.

In the first of the aphorisms of "Wisdom of the Unfinished," Frey articulates in existential terms—"Why should I live in such a way that it makes sense to die?" (p. 38)—a position that, translated into the general terms of the book, might look like a blueprint for its production: Why should I write in such a way that it makes sense to end? But for the project of "fragmentary writing" to succeed, this cannot be understood as a programmatic statement. As Frey argues in "Living Fragmentarily," one cannot *choose* fragmentariness as an attitude, since fragmentariness is the absence of elements or reference points that would render a choice possible. Thus, the aphorism that names the project of fragmentariness also disavows it as a project by taking the form of a question, which, as we know from the two texts on "Asking," is one only as long as it remains open. To the extent that *Interruptions* can be said to make fragmentariness into a project, to choose to renounce mastery, and to answer its own question, it is not fragmentary in Frey's sense. But in putting the project in question at every turn it comes very close to being able to ask about the fragment without systematically violating its resistance: in an accidental, open-ended, and paradoxical way.

Among those who have helped ensure that this project would come to an end, I wish to thank Philip Leider, Matthew Potolsky, and especially Franziska Gross, Elizabeth Rottenberg, and Andrzej Warminski. Thanks also to Rodolphe Gasché, Werner Hamacher, and Kevin Newmark, who made this possible in the first place, and to Hans-Jost Frey: for his unfailing support.

Georgia Albert

Interruptions

by
Hans-Jost Frey

STORIES

Interruptions

- ● Here we are, talking again. As though we still had something to say to each other. It seems that we cannot get away from each other.
- ○ We don't know each other.
- ● But we need each other . . .
- ○ Neither of us is complete.
- ● . . . without the other. We complement each other.
- ○ Aren't we talking right past each other?
- ● Aren't you overshooting the mark there?
- ○ That's just what I was saying.
- ● I still hope that we'll understand each other some day.
- ○ Maybe we will some time. But when we understand each other, we don't understand *each other*. I don't understand you or you me. What we understand, we have in common, but what we would like to make understood—what you are and what I am—is precisely what we cannot have in common.
- ● If we can only say what we have in common, then no conversation, no matter how long, can help us get to know each other. And yet we only talk because we are separated and would like to get beyond that.
- ○ That's what we have in common . . .
- ● . . . and we can come to an understanding about it. Yes. But what is in common could be said by one of us for both. We don't need a dialogue for that. My talking to you and your talking to me, that is still something else than reveling in what we have in common, even if this common element were only our insight into our being irreparably separated. It is not the same if two talk or only one. The difference . . .
- ○ . . . consists in this, that if there are two people each person can only ever talk when the other lets him.

- So why don't you let me finish talking?
○ Because we are in conversation and conversation is perhaps this: that one does not finish talking. Or that one does not talk oneself into believing that one can finish talking, as preachers and teachers do, whose worth and credibility seems to depend on the fact that they are beyond the pupil, who is "unfinished." In conversation one talks in such a way that the other also has something to say. Does that not mean that one stops talking at some point in order to let the other speak, or that the other speaks up when he has something to say? Conversation is interruption.
- One comes across people—and it is true that many teachers are among them—who talk constantly. Then one says that they lecture. But the unceasing flow of speech does not indicate that someone has more to say than someone else. In the continuous talk the fear of stopping also speaks, the horror at the silence that follows my words and lets the Other *[das Andere]* arise, the Other that one has to take into account without being able to count on it. The chatterer's flood of words is a way to fend off conversation through the Danaid-like effort to fill all of the holes out of which the other person could speak.
○ Then only the one who gives up the idea of leading the conversation would be suited to having one. Conversation is always abrupt, whatever efforts we make to connect what we say to what the other has said. In conversation we always work at covering up the breach that allows us to speak to each other. We seek unanimity, as though what matters were not precisely what has no place in unity because it constitutes me or you. True, the fact that you talk and what you say creates, in some respects, a connection between us, but it also undermines the illusion of my integrity, which I, to the extent that I am alone, carry around with me. By the mere fact that it takes place, your talking is an objection against monologue, it is contradiction without your needing to speak against me, in it speaks

6

what does not belong to me and that to which I don't belong, the disquieting, not assimilable . . . you . . . it . . . what interrupts me . . . into which I break off . . .

● While you were talking, you looked out the window into the rain, and I observed your profile. It is jagged like a shard. Whatever beautiful and comforting things may be said about the human face: it also has the fortuitousness of the breaking point. I mean less a broken cup—which one could glue together again—than a mountainous horizon. No one would think of restoring the mountains to wholeness like an ancient vase, although one also cannot claim that they are whole as they are. The mountain-climber who believes himself to be at the top really is only at the place where it stops—not at the end of the world but where it breaks off. Our noses are mountains, and our faces are to each other like mountain landscapes, but without ever interlocking the way teeth do in a mouth. No one can make it beyond his own skyline, and it is only the unbridgeable gaps between us that talk about what we cannot say to each other.

○ Sometimes, though, one believes one is getting beyond the tip of one's nose. Perhaps this happens most readily when one is interrupted. Then one can no longer give in to the temptation to take oneself to be whole. Each interruption opens a crack in the shell that one builds around oneself with sentences, and one is born into one's own unfinishedness. Being unfinished I am finally open to that which never reaches me.

● Behind the unbroken shell Narcissus waits for himself. But the egg that protects him does not let him develop, and when he is born he loses himself unless Sleeping Beauty frees him.

Nanteos

In its Welsh secludedness, Nanteos is a stately, but not really outstanding, example of those English mansions that are opened by their impoverished owners to the curiosity of paying tourists who would like to experience the way the wealthy used to live. While in most of these houses the former distinction has stiffened into a museum-like stage set, which one looks into from over silken cordons, here the gaze comes from inside, and Nanteos soaks it up into itself. To the mood that lies here belong the threadbare carpets, the pale-brittle covers on the armchairs, the scraps of paint that peel off where the walls are damp, and all the other signs of decay, but also, and just as much, the effort to conjure up a vision of the everyday life of the former residents down to the smallest detail. The table is set and the carafe filled with wine; on the sideboard is a basket with the right number of napkins, ready in monogrammed silver rings. The beds are made and one can use the old-fashioned toilet. The illusion that people live here—that one almost lives here oneself—is complete and at the same time becomes blurred over and over again in the traces of dissolution.

Outlived life lives on here, not as a quiet image of former comfort, but unwanted and disturbing. The life in this house seems to have forgotten to stop although it has long been out of place, and has become uncanny. There is not too little in this house, although it is falling apart, but too much. The excess that does not belong here, that which is over without having come to an end, or which has come to an end without quite being over, the unredeemed which continues to be even after it is no longer: the ghostly.

Abyss

Right behind the village is the abyss. The village itself is actually unworthy of note, the houses are like anywhere else, and precisely because everything is so ordinary a special effort is needed to locate the impression of something extraordinary that the village makes right from the start. Since it has no church, it lacks a middle around which people otherwise like to settle, and since there is also no cemetery, nothing leads to the conclusion that the people here are born or die. They are unforeseeably there—or not, as the case may be. That no great importance is attached to this question depends on the proximity of the abyss. Not that it is taken particularly seriously or, much less, thought of as something threatening. On the contrary, a great peace seems to come from it. The people's faces are clear and simple, their manner carefree but not reckless, and they behave to each other with an indifference that has nothing offensive about it, because it is always full of consideration. No one is offensive to others and no one has anything to hide. Everyone respects the other's right, which is also his own. It is hardly spoken about, since it is never at issue. The only right that there is here is the right to the abyss, and no court is needed to enforce it. The abyss is too close for that. Everyone can get to it easily by following the path behind the village. When someone dies, he is taken there, but many also go there before their time and step out, and those who remain know that they, too, have a right to do that. When they talk about it, it is without pathos. Those who go into the abyss do not take their leave, since they do not leave anything any more than when they go to bed at night. The foreigners that come to the village every now and then, bringing false hopes with them, leave again when they see through their misunderstanding, or stay if they find a way to relate to the abyss and to the fact that one does not die in it. The hope that someone places in the fall, or the fear that another, the same one, has of it, has nothing to do with the abyss, but only with the bottom on which some imagine that the fall ends. The abyss has no bottom. One does not fall in it. When one falls, one always falls towards the center. The abyss frees from the center. Once someone tried to disrupt the peace of the village by affirming that it could not be proven that the abyss really is the abyss, since, as he said, one cannot know whether it might not, after all, have a bottom somewhere. He was given to understand, however, that precisely the impossibility and needlessness of this decision is the abyss.

"No . . ." Sign

At the crossing of two forest trails was a prohibition sign. Children had clearly used it repeatedly as a target, and where the rocks had knocked off the paint, rust stains spread, and the writing underneath had become unreadable. Thus it was impossible to decide what was not allowed, although the word "No . . ." could still be clearly deciphered. The sign should have been replaced long before, and that this was not happening indicated, perhaps, that the prohibition was not meant too seriously or was not very important. Against that, however, spoke the fact that the sign had been put up in the first place and that, even now that it did not fulfill its task adequately, it had not yet been removed, a fact understood by most people as meaning that the prohibition was as valid as ever. Although some claimed that it had been left there out of negligence, and that no one needed to worry about it anymore, even they didn't know for sure. In general one tried to elude the pressure of the prohibition by referring it to things that one would not have thought of doing anyway. Those who liked to walk in the forest were convinced that horseback riding was forbidden, while the riders maintained that dogs were not to be let free; the dog owners in their turn held mushroom-gathering to be unlawful. But these were only attempts to relieve one's own conscience, since no action was free from the suspicion of being forbidden anymore. The sign could mean any action, and it was no longer possible to do anything with the certainty that it was allowed. The consequence of this distressing uncertainty was that gradually fewer and fewer people went to this part of the forest, as though it had been a forbidden place. In the meantime it's all grown wild here and the sign is almost overgrown. However, children must still have been throwing rocks here at some point, because where earlier the "o" could still be made out there is now a hole.

Law

Our country has no borders. Not that it would be too large for that, but it is right next to No Man's Land, and no one quite knows where it turns into it. Travelers who visit us are there all of a sudden, without being able to tell where they entered the country. Yet no one except for them is surprised by this. We are not concerned with the extension of the national territory, and our population statistics, too, are hardly an object of interest for anyone. When someone goes away, his absence is not felt, except of course by those who are close to him, and immigrants don't concern us, although we don't need them.

Our history fades into uncertainty, since no research is done on it, and since we feel no need for a past that would explain us. We don't know, after all, whether anything ever began. We also don't have a national holiday—the criteria by which to decide on an important date are not sure enough.

Although in our country everything grows blurred on the edges, we do have laws. It is true that strictly speaking no one knows what is allowed and what is forbidden, but we must live, and therefore our life together has to be regulated somehow. However, our laws, if they want to be taken seriously, can only be formulated and promulgated with the awareness that they don't cover every case and are therefore insufficient. The law is only acceptable if it takes its own provisional character into account and, since it is not definitive, it also does not decree anything that would be irrevocable. Being provisional, it remains endlessly open to modification and it is never binding in its present form, but must be put into question again and again, although it should also be in force at the same time. The law never *is:* it is always in progress. Perhaps the unrelenting attempt to formulate it is the only way in which it takes effect. In any case the only sensible way to apply it is not to cling to it. The law does not relieve anybody of responsibility.

The endeavor not to set down in the law more than we can take responsibility for with a good conscience makes it difficult (since in the final analysis we can take responsibility for very little) to give the law weight, because the police and army can never be employed with full conviction to maintain an order that remains inadequate in so many respects. It would be simpler to declare the law definitive and enforce it uncompromisingly, but then, it has always been an unwritten law that the law is only necessary to the extent that it isn't sufficient. We would no longer have any use for a law that would protect the interests of every one of us. The law serves us only to the extent that it always also fails at the same time. This is our difficulty: we know that the law is inadequate, which is why we can uphold it only if we also constantly work on its improvement; but we also know that since we change the law all the time we can only uphold it tepidly, because in fact it is always already outdated. When the law is violated, that is of course on the one hand an offense that we punish, since disrespect has been shown to the law's claim to validity, without which it cannot be what it is; on the other hand, the violation is an indication of the insufficiency of the law within whose framework some fallible person has not been able to cope. That's why when a culprit is punished the law is changed at the same time. The way this is done is that he has to stand up for his interests and take part in reforming the law. The lawbreaker serves his sentence as a lawgiver. Thus he stops being a criminal, but the new law possibly causes discontent in others, who will perhaps let themselves be carried away into committing unlawful actions.

We are never secure and our nation has no stability, but that we don't pretend it has any is its strength.

Surprise

The Bureau for Unforeseen Events is attached to the Department of Planning. Its area of competence is not always understood correctly, and so it happens all the time that people report to this office on the assumption that it concerns itself with all that cannot be included in the planning. In a certain sense this is also true, but it would be mistaken to construe the creation of the Bureau as an act of modesty on the part of the Department of Planning. The existence of the Bureau does not in any way indicate the acceptance of the unforeseeable: on the contrary, it is a measure aimed at increasing foresight. The task of the Bureau is, if not the abolition, then the greatest possible limitation of the unforeseen, which is felt to be a disturbance and a bother. While it is true that all the unforeseen events that come to our attention are collected here, this is only done in order that the competent officials may deliberate on how to include them in future planning. Once a wealthy industrialist, having decided to make a donation to the orphanage, made inquiries at the Bureau for Unforeseen Events, since it seemed to him that his gift could hardly be expected. Precisely for this reason, it was made clear to him, the gift could not be accepted without further ado—there would soon be trouble for law and order if everybody was allowed to plan surprises of this sort. It was pointed out to him that the gift, of all things, is something questionable in the extreme, since the giver puts himself every time in a position of superiority by way of the fact that the recipient is deprived of the possibility of preparing for the gift and is therefore left defenseless, at the mercy of every passing fancy. It was decided to make gifts subject to previous approval in order to make it possible to include them in the planning and thus deprive them of their dangerous potential.

With time it became more and more obvious that only total expectation offered protection against the unforeseen, and that in order not to be taken by surprise one had to be ready for everything. It would be easy to eliminate the danger of being surprised if one were only ready not to have any specific expectations. One who was prepared for anything would always have included the unforeseen in the plans, too, and would no longer be affected by it. An unprejudiced employee of the Bureau, however, took these considerations further and reasoned that that would mean letting everything out of one's hands and putting oneself at the mercy of any event that might occur, so that abolishing surprise would also paralyze planning—which in fact, he concluded, was itself the cause of all the problems in the first place. Planning, he affirmed, was a mistake and should be given up. Only when one had become indifferent toward the future and no longer wanted to shape it would the fear of the unforeseen also go away. When he presented these thoughts, he was given to understand that the simultaneous abolition of the unforeseen and of planning would plunge us into chaos, while the patient reporting of all irregularities to higher authorities on the part of the Bureau for Unforeseen Events did not allow the faith in the possibility of planning to waver and ensured the smooth cooperation of the governmental offices.

In this explanation lay the unintended confession of our dependence on the unforeseen—of the fact that, for example, no project for an orphanage could be drafted if the parents' demise could be planned in advance. Since then, planning has had to forfeit some of its unquestioned self-assurance. The possibility that at some point it might be overtaken by the feeling of its own futility has never quite left the halls of the Department. Even more stress than before is laid on how large a threat is posed by the unforeseen, which the planning lives on, and the Bureau for Unforeseen Events has been instructed to be especially alert so that nothing might escape its control. In the face of these self-preserving measures any attempt to give serious consideration to closing down the Department of Planning would be a surprise.

Signposts

Until not long ago it was difficult to find one's way around our region. Where there was more than one way to go one could only make a hit-or-miss choice. Since one somehow always "hit," nobody complained about it. It happened again and again that even people who weren't familiar with the area reached their destination by taking the risk of the unknown road without hesitation: they entrusted themselves to its meanderings, feeling like pioneers. Recently the administration, in an effort to gain the favor of the population, had signs put up at all junctions and intersections in order to end this state of uncertainty, which it considered outrageous and untenable. It has since become clear to everyone who has been in the position of reading the new signs that all the roads lead to our capital. This was of course (or perhaps) always the case, but we didn't know it so clearly. Now it is as if the state had been simplified to a skeleton and we could see its anatomy. No one is quite so eager to start out on a journey anymore. Ever since the destination has been posted everywhere the roads have lost much of their appeal, because it no longer makes any difference which one you choose. Some ask themselves what may have induced the administration to lay bare the structure of the road network in so revealing a way. The motives have remained unclear, although some particularly angry people demonstrated in the streets with banners that demanded "More Transparency!" The administration explained that it had had this very wish in mind, but it also admitted not to have realized where its willingness to provide information would lead. At the moment they are still deliberating whether the signposts should be removed again. But whether or not this happens will hardly make a difference, since now we know where the roads all lead anyway. The best thing would be to leave the signs where they are until an official decides, hit or miss, to have them taken away.

Asking i

I am waiting for you. I hope you will come. But will you come? It is uncertain. I doubt it. I have been waiting too long. I can no longer fill the time. Waiting is boring. What am I waiting for anyway? And how can I wait if I don't know what I am waiting for? I don't know whether I am waiting for something anymore. But I *am* waiting! Am I really waiting? Don't I even know that I am waiting anymore? How could I be waiting? After all, I don't have anything I could be waiting for. That's why I am bored. But why do I ask so many questions when I am bored? If what I am asking about interests me, I am not bored. Is it uncertain, then, whether I am bored? Right now I am interested in this question: whether I am bored. How can I finally put an end to this asking? I must give myself an answer instead of always asking. But the reason I ask is that I can't answer. Can I at least answer the question "Why can't I answer"? Because I don't have the answer. But that still does not mean that there is no answer. It takes patience— precisely. Maybe the answer will turn up some time. I am waiting for it. I hope it will come. But will it come? It is uncertain, and I doubt it sometimes. I've waited so long already! What am I waiting for anyway? Now the questions are starting again. The reason for that is that the answer is missing. In order for this to finally change, something would have to happen. But nothing happens. Is it really true that nothing happens? Nothing is happening now, but it may be of course that something will happen some time. That's what I am waiting for. I hope it will happen. But will it happen? Until it hap- pens—should it ever happen—I can only wait and ask. I wait, asking, and ask, waiting. What for? What about? For something to happen that will end my waiting and still my asking. But nothing happens. That's why I wait and ask. Only this. But this happens. It has hap- pened the whole time. I have waited in the question. I am waiting in it. What am I waiting for? That something else than that which happens as a question may happen. Since this other thing is not in the question, I ask about it. I wait for it and hope that it will happen. But it is uncertain, this other thing. Perhaps it is nowhere but in the asking about it. Then I have it precisely when I don't have it and ask about it. If it is so, then I must continue to ask in order to keep it as that which I don't have. If it isn't so, and the other thing happens as an answer beyond the question, I must also continue to ask in order to await it. It is uncertain whether the other of the question exists or not. That's precisely why I ask about it. But I don't *ask*, actually: I only affirm that I ask. In the affirmation of the asking the question is lost. I want to look for it. But is the question something that one can look for and find, something that one can ask about and that one can give in an answer? Just now the question was there—in the question about it whose sound has just faded. But not as answer, as question. Now that I can say that it was still there just now, it is no longer here. Can only a question be the answer to the question about the question? It is uncertain. That's why I ask. I wait in the question. Until the answer comes. Maybe it won't come. Then I'll wait long, longer and longer, until I can no longer fill the time. What am I waiting for? For time to pass . . . waiting . . . talking . . . asking . . .

End

He said that the fact that it was over now [*dass es jetzt fertig sei*] meant only that they had not gotten over it [*dass sie damit nicht fertig geworden seien*]. What one cannot get over, he said, goes on in its tormenting incompletion [*Unfertigkeit*], which no level of accomplishment [*keine Fertigkeit*] could hope to cope with. Should she have drawn the conclusion from the fact that they couldn't get over each other that they had reached the end, he could only laugh at that, since what could possibly be the end of incompleteness—besides, at most, a neverending end in death. There was no end for them, he said, and their rapport was infinite precisely because it was so utterly unfinished. Of course they could break off the relationship, but by doing that they would forfeit whatever hope there still was of ever bringing it to an end, because the break, far from being an end, only subjected them to the definitive impossibility of ever putting an end to it . . .

She could not find anything to answer to that. It seemed to her that there was no question. The tension between them was intolerable, but that was precisely the reason why she was unable to end it. She could never come closer to the end [*Ende*] than its rhymes as they occurred to her: walls [*Wände*] full of volumes [*Bände*] of rhymes without end— they are all too easy to understand [*man kann sie mit Händen greifen*], but they are good for nothing, only for talking on.

Volcano

- We live on a volcano and wait for it to erupt. We know that it will happen, and the geologists who constantly take measurements even say that it can't be long now. But perhaps they are just deluding us in order to help us, since they know that we cannot bear this immemorial wait anymore. It is not just that we are waiting for the volcano to erupt: the waiting itself is the volcano in us. The eruption—that would be anything that would happen so that we would not have to wait anymore. We would welcome anything; the worst as well as the best would at least ease the tension of the wait, which has long become intolerable, but we have had to learn that this is not enough to produce an explosion. No matter how steadfastly and how long we wait, our waiting engenders nothing but the impossibility of standing it any longer. With this impossibility we must live—without being able to.

- Others have talked this way before. To me this sounds like a clumsy imitation. And what gives you the right to say "we," anyway? It seems to me that one can only speak in one's own name.

- I agree with you. I thought I was talking in the name of those who wait. But precisely because I did it I could not claim that I was doing it anymore, since those who wait do not talk, they wait, while in me talking erupted. But what should I care? Those who have never waited may worry about it.

BREAK-OFF

Ending Beginning

Here is now here. But however true that still was a moment ago, now *here* is already there, at the beginning, and instead of it something else was—and now, again, no longer is—here. That *here* is at the beginning can also only be true when the beginning is no longer here. The beginning is there and in retrospect. *Here* and *now* are words with which one can only lie. The beginning, which exists only after the fact, has always already been the beginning. There is no such thing as beginning, only having begun, and it remains unclear how it has come to that.

At that time a hunt started: the letters have been trying to catch up with the Here and the Now, from which they get further and further away even as they are formed. The text writes itself towards the beginning, which slips away from it more and more precisely for this reason. The more the text strives towards its goal—to be able to begin— the more it is already beyond it, past it in time and space *[jenseitig, jenzeitig]*.

What, having begun, cannot begin, cannot end. The end would be the chance to begin, which the text endlessly misses by going on. Just as the beginning lies before as well as behind, so does the end lie behind as well as before. Because the end cannot be said, saying can have no end. Where the text ends it is unfinished, because although its end has come it is still unsaid, and when the text says it, it has not yet come to an end, since it is still in the middle of saying that it has. Writing, which must always already have begun in order to be able to say that it has, must always continue in order to be able to say that it is ending. It always ends too early or too late, and therefore does not end at all, for it misses its own end.

23

Language can begin and end, but it cannot, beginning, say the beginning and, ending, say the end. Beginning and end cannot be controlled, and that makes it impossible for anything ever to be whole. That something begins and ends is not meaningful while it happens, and can be justified only retrospectively, as talking goes on.

The ideal of the whole endangers meaning, since it would like to enclose meaning out of fear of meaning's borders. Since meaning depends on the fact that talking goes on, the ideal of the whole, the hope to get the end under control by concluding, is an illusion that, deceiving, drives on the quest for meaning. The whole pretends to be immune against that which is outside of it. But by striving to exclude meaninglessness from itself, the whole exposes itself to it: its blindness to its own position in its surroundings, its very disregard for them, makes it powerless against them.

The arbitrariness of beginning and end, which are impossible to keep a watch on from the inside of the whole, is the whole's crumbling away at the edges.

Fragment and Whole

Understanding the fragment would mean: giving it meaning. The fragment has meaning when it can be brought into a context within which it fulfills a task. But the fragment is what it is precisely because there is no context for it. No whole can accommodate it. The breaking point of the fragment is the edge of meaning. Thus the fragment seems to be hostile to meaning and resists understanding. All the attempts to explain it turn it into something it is not and end up in contradiction with their own aim. To the extent that they succeed, they disavow the fragmentariness of the fragment and treat it as a whole or as part of a whole, because this is the only way to bring what is incomplete into a context.

Understanding the fragment means: understanding its incompleteness. The fragment has meaning when its incompleteness essentially belongs to it, that is, when what we have takes such a form that it becomes evident from it that and why the fragment could not achieve completeness. However, when the fragment contains in itself the reason why it is unfinished, it stops being a fragment. Incompleteness, when it acquires meaning, is no longer what breaks up the context but is brought back into it. As expression of the impossibility of completion, the incompleteness of the alleged fragment is precisely what brings it to its completion as all it can be, and thus makes it into a whole. Now the fragment has been understood—but only at the expense of its fragmentariness.

The other way to understand the fragment would consist in finding external, rather than internal, reasons for its incompleteness. If the fragment has remained unfinished not out of internal necessity but because of external factors, then it cannot be understood on its own terms, and because no attempt is made to extract its meaning from it only, it is also not bent forcibly into a whole. But the openness that the fragment is allowed to keep in this way only leads to a higher closure. If understanding the fragment from inside is now impossible, it becomes nonetheless possible to understand it through the external circumstances that have prevented its completion. The fragmentary character of the fragment acquires meaning in the context of these circumstances. Although the fragment is now no longer treated as whole, it is treated as part of a larger structure of meaning from which it cannot be detached.

Understanding the fragment thus always means: integrating it. Depending on whether one attributes the incompleteness of the fragment to internal or external reasons, one makes it into a whole or into a part of a whole. One understands the fragment at the expense of its fragmentary nature. Understanding is precisely the suppression of fragmentariness, since it creates context where every relation breaks off.

The fragment is neither a whole nor a part. This means that it cannot be understood from the perspective of the whole. The archeologist who glues potsherds together and the dentist who fills cavities have no sense for the fragmentary, and just as little does the philosopher who tries to construct a system out of fragments. They are all nostalgic for wholeness and flee from what they cannot master into the security of closure. But the openness of the fragment is not temporary and cannot be repaired. If it were a whole the fragment would not be a fragment anymore; if it were a part it could be completed and made into a whole. Because it is neither a whole nor a part, it remains resistant to closure. An encounter with it is possible only when the whole, as a structure of meaning accessible to the understanding, is no longer a possibility: outside the whole, where the whole is not even no longer there, but fades into oblivion.

Against the fragment's independence from the whole the objection can be raised that outside the whole there is nothing. The whole outside of which there is still something else is thought of as being finite. But because if something is finite it is always possible to add something to it in thought, nothing finite is ever the whole, or better, it is not whole in the sense of totality. Nonetheless, something finite can be whole—not in the sense that there is nothing left outside of it, but in the sense that it contains in itself everything that belongs to it. Wholeness is the order in which everything has its place and in which nothing is missing or excessive. Inside the order of the finite whole everything is a part, which means that everything is recognizable in its relationship to the whole and is therefore read as a metonymy for the whole. But this storing of the parts in the whole is as satisfactory as the position of the whole is disquieting. The whole, if it is finite, is not all-encompassing and remains surrounded by everything that has no place in its order. As soon as this unmastered remainder against the claim to closure made by order is perceived, the question arises whether the finite whole is again, in its turn, part of a higher whole. The whole that includes everything and outside of which there is nothing—the whole about which, therefore, this question need no longer be asked—is the infinite whole. If it is assumed to be ordered, then everything that is, is a part and has meaning to the extent that it contributes to the whole in an incomprehensible, but believed-in, order. If the infinite whole is made dependent on this assumption— and does this not already mean that this assumption is once again outside of the whole?—then the fragment does not exist, because there is nothing but the whole and its parts. If however the whole is not an order, but just simply everything, then nothing of what is found inside it is a part, because it is not related to something else together with which it forms a context. Every order is then only human fiction and not knowledge of what is. Everything is fragment because it is neither whole nor part, and all ordering is a vain attempt to make fragments into parts. The infinite whole onto which one does not stick the label of order as though it were a bottle whose content could be described appears, through the waning human conception of wholeness, in its pale neutrality: as the outside where the illusion of order is invalidated.

Every discourse on fragmentariness that evades the question whether the infinite whole is to be thought of as an order or not does not come anywhere near its object and cannot even decide whether this object exists at all. And indeed this decision must be suspended as long as the question whether the infinite whole is ordered remains open. The impossibility of answering it constitutes the difficulty of the fragment, since one does not even know whether it is one or whether perhaps it can, after all, be conceived of as part of a whole. But the habit of wanting to understand is so powerful that the question about the infinite whole has mostly been decided—in favor of order—before it is asked. Every attempt to understand always already makes the assumption that there is a meaning there that can be determined. One posits order before having it. The reductive understanding of the fragment from the point of view of the order of whole and parts bears witness to this tacit presupposition of order. In order to open up a space for the fragmentary even as mere possibility it is therefore first of all necessary to undermine the unquestioned assurance with which wholeness and context are postulated. It is only when the possibility that it might be otherwise is considered that the fragmentary nature of the fragment can finally come into view. The concern with this question shows that the belief in the order of the whole is recognized as unproven and is no longer taken as a basis. The collapse of the belief in the meaning of the whole does not mean a profession of faith in disorder, since to affirm disorder would be as impossible to justify as the hope to do away with it. In the face of the fragment, which puts wholeness in question, it is neither possible to give up wanting to understand nor certain whether the quest for meaning is meaningful. Here the doubting of meaning accompanies the quest for it.

Limit of the Possible

One may be tempted to separate fragments into necessary and accidental ones. Necessarily fragmentary is what by its essence cannot
be whole, while the accidental fragment has remained unfinished
because of circumstances that have nothing to do with it. The necessary fragment will easily be regarded as the only one worth inves-
tigating, the accidental one set aside as "inauthentic." And this precisely
to the extent that confrontation with the fragmentary is avoided over
and over again. For it is not just the priority given to one kind over
the other that does not hold, but the differentiation itself. Nothing
is essentially unfinished. That which, by its essence, cannot be finished
fulfills its essence by remaining unfinished and is thereby whole. Its
incompletion is in this case explainable and understandable: it stops
where it should, at the end. This cannot be said of the accidental
fragment. It breaks off before becoming what it was meant to be. A
poem remains incomplete because the poet has died. But it is mere
claim to call this death an accident, just as it would be, inversely, equally
arbitrary to want to prove that it had to occur at this very moment.
Thus the necessary fragment is no fragment anymore, and the accidental fragment may not be accidental at all. The necessary fragment
is understandable at the expense of fragmentariness (and that is why
it is preferred), the accidental fragment remains fragmentary at the
expense of understanding. But no understanding of the fragmentary
can be based on the opposition of necessity and accident.

It can neither be said of the fragment that it is necessary nor that it
is accidental. It disables this opposition. Or to say this differently:
the breaking point of the fragment is the boundary of the possible.
This boundary is not reached only here. A whole, too, can come up
to the limit of the possible, but then no urge arises to get beyond the
boundary, since even what is outermost is held from the center and

remains dependent on it. In the case of the fragment the crossing of the boundary is unavoidable, because the boundary of the possible here does not mark the contour of the whole, but the unfinishedness that one must, but cannot, get beyond. The breaking point is the fall into impossibility and its lack of oppositions. The impossibility that becomes visible in the fragment is not simply the negation of possibility. It is the more-than-possible as the reality of the impossible. The fragmentary is the experience that the boundary of the possible is drawn closer than that of the real.

We move mostly inside the possible, do what we can, build for ourselves a world in which we can live. But there are breaks, break-ins in this order, states of the outer limit that are, however, unfulfilled, that one cannot get beyond though everything urges beyond them. I call them fragmentary states. They are the everyday experience of the impossible.

The significance of the fragment for literature should be looked for in the fact that the literary text, even when it grows into a whole, is perhaps that whole which traces its origin back to the limit of the possible.

Paradox

Literary scholarship (*Literaturwissenschaft*) concerns itself with the works as finished products, as texts that lack nothing and in which nothing is superfluous. When one believes one can show this, a reassuring wholeness begins to appear, a wholeness that one would like to be without remainder—which is why any remainder is ignored as much as possible. The usual aim of talking about texts is to understand the text as order and thus to make it accessible to the grasp of the concept. That is why the fragment, which does not fulfill the presupposition of wholeness, is not a popular object for literary scholarship and perhaps not even a possible one. The fragment cannot be controlled. Thus the encounter of literary scholarship with the fragment creates a contradictory situation. Either the discourse about the fragment must deny it as what it is and falsely make it into a whole, or it must itself be put into question in its claim to master the text. Either the fragment or literary scholarship must be given up.

The paradoxical tension of this situation is no reason to stop talking. Although it becomes especially apparent when one deals with the fragment, this tension is covertly at work in every form of talking about texts that, insofar as it wants to make them into something that can be understood and controlled, starts from the assumption that they are not. If the texts need to be explained, then they are lacking; if they do not, then their refusal to be brought under control is an essential part of them. In the first case the wholeness of the text is compromised, in the second the attempt to master it is in contradiction with it. This contradiction breaks out in connection with the fragment. One cannot talk about the fragment with the intent of making it into something that one can control. Here it is unavoidable that the illusion of the mastery-producing statement of fact, into which the discourse that speaks in affirmative clauses slides over and over again, should be dismantled. The fragment can only be approached by a discourse without claim to power.

Discourse makes available and functions through the production of relations that can be logical or rhetorical in nature. What is brought into an argumentative or affective context is arranged into an order and therefore is understandable. What makes the fragmentary—and generally the literary—text resistant to control is that not everything can be captured in relationships. What cannot be mastered in texts is what cannot be integrated, what cannot be absorbed by either a logical or a rhetorical relation: what is unrelated. Since discourse is relation, it is impossible to talk about the fragment, unless any relation that inevitably arises from the moment that there is talking is also immediately dissolved, since it does not hold any more than any other one, which is in its turn also posited [gesetzt] only so that it can be deposed [zersetzt]. The kind of talking that does not try to make relations available relies on the paradox, the rhetorical figure that, by asserting contradiction, announces the neutralization of logic. The paradox posits the impossible relation and thereby points out of the possibility of relation and toward what is unrelated, incomprehensible, unmasterable. Yet the paradox attains the unmasterable only indirectly, because it still makes use of the irreconcilability of opposites and thus has not yet reached the point where logic no longer rules. The paradox belongs to a discourse that still speaks from inside logic, although at its border and away from it, and tries to get beyond logic with logic's own means.

Any discourse on the fragment that is not simply reductive becomes paradoxical. Seen from the perspective of a repressive literary scholarship this is its "weakness," but thanks to this weakness it can come close to its object without having to coincide with it and break off.

Asking ii

It is wholeness that is in question for the one who asks. He asks so that the answer may reconstitute it for him. The close connection of question and answer easily covers up the state of unfinishedness in which the questioner finds himself. The question is seen so much from the perspective of the answer that it only appears as an instrument of cognition. This intimate conjunction of question and answer is dominated by the assumption that the answer is inseparable from the question. But it does not belong to the essence of the question that it can be answered. The unanswerable question does not stop being a question; on the contrary it is the fact that the answer does not come that upholds it in its asking. But if there is such a thing as a question without answer, then the question must be thought of independently of the answer. Not, however, as though the unanswerable question were a question of a special kind. Just as any other question, it too looks ahead toward the answer. If one knew that there was no answer, one would not ask. The question is uncertain about the knowledge that it asks for. Not just the content of the answer is uncertain, however: it is also uncertain whether there is any answer. The question opens up a gap about which it is not certain whether it can be closed again. It shares the risk of the fragment.

To ask in order to know is to call for an answer. This asking is not present to itself, but always already beyond itself, with the expected answer. It is an asking that is not satisfied with itself, but aims at its own dismissal in the obtained knowledge. It can happen, however, that the answer is long in coming. Then the asking is left to itself, and it becomes clear that it is precisely not to be understood from the perspective of knowledge, but is, on the contrary, the expression of non-knowledge. There can only be question when knowledge is lacking. Thus the question is at the same time an appeal for what it does not know and a confession of the lack of this knowledge. As the mode of appearance of non-knowledge, the question becomes the form of expression of the skeptic: it helps him avoid the affirmative clause, which must always assert a knowledge. The sentence "I know nothing" still says the knowledge of non-knowledge: "I know that I know nothing," a knowledge that is put into question in its turn in the question "What do I know?" The question is the possibility of saying one's non-knowledge without making it again into a knowledge. Non-knowledge exists only in the process of asking the question. The skeptic's question does not primarily ask in order to know; rather, it puts knowing into question. Nevertheless the question "What do I know?" explicitly asks about what I know. Perhaps there is even an answer to this question, and this possibility must always be kept in mind, because the question can only ask in the suspended space of uncertainty, only so long as neither knowing nor its impossibility is certain. This uncertainty belongs to the essence of the question.

The answer can be long in coming. Then, the question persists in its asking. The more it persists, the more asking becomes waiting. In the wait, it is no longer only the question or the answer that matters, but what is between them. The more this space in between extends, the more the question becomes a mere opening onto a lack and the more the hope of getting an answer decreases. Thus the wait becomes more and more boring, but it remains an asking all the same, because the uncertainty about whether the answer will come is preserved and preserves the question, no matter how much thinner, weaker, and more colorless the question becomes. The question pales as the lack onto which it opens gains the upper hand. The emptiness of this lack is not negativity, because in it the answer is not denied, but pending. It is uncertain whether there is an answer or not. The question's opening itself into uncertainty can be no particular expectation of an answer, since perhaps the answer does not exist. However, it is also not an empty waiting, a no longer goal-driven one, since such a waiting would no longer be an asking but mere persistence in the impossibility of an answer. All certainty is beyond the question. However, although the impossibility of an answer is never certain so long as the question asks, there is a hopeless asking. At some point the asking stops being the expectation of an answer and the hope of getting an answer disappears. The question loses its direction and yet keeps asking. The uncertainty lasts so long that the thought of its opposite gradually fades away and makes it become unmeasurable. Imperceptibly, gradually, the asking forgets the answer.

To understand the question as directed toward an answer is to obscure it. But detaching the question from the answer also gives no access to it, for it is always in order to know that one asks about the question. One asks about the question to acquire certainty about uncertainty. The question about the question calls for an answer. But how could the essence of the question be contained in an answer? This would mean that the essence of the question is not to be found in the question itself, that the question is inessential and that the answer is, after all, the most important thing. If, however, the essence of the question is found in its asking, no answer can grasp it. The question about the question is then just as futile as the endeavor to answer it. Nowhere but in asking does the question disclose itself: not in the asking *about* the question, but in the asking *of* the question.

Asserting

The assertion establishes groundlessly. That it is ungrounded is what makes it into an assertion in the first place. Of course one can always trace it back to something, but in the inquiries that make this possible the fear that perhaps it may not be possible is also at work. One doesn't like just to leave the assertion there. When it cannot be grounded and thereby connected to something known, it is denounced as inadequate, because it cannot prove the claim it makes that it is telling the truth. This bothers those who are concerned about the impact of its content, and who live in the conviction that one should only be allowed to say what one can take responsibility for, since it could always happen that one will have to take responsibility for it. But any speaker, as speaker, has to stand by things he cannot take responsibility for. When one starts to speak, one asserts by breaking the silence. The fact that someone speaks, independently of what is said, is assertion, and whether or not the assertion is correct is less important than the fact that it, as unconcerned positing, does not try to hush up the abrupt and ir-responsible beginning of all speaking. The assertion is the fragment that does not break off where it stops but where and by the fact that it begins. What is asserted has no roots. One can only assert where the context is missing. The assertion, even when it asserts context, is the tacit renunciation of wholeness. So long as assertions are made, there is no completed work, which is perhaps why in the end the work is only an assertion. Should the world have been created, it would be God's assertion. Every retrospective attempt to justify the assertion does not realize that its strength lies in its *gratuité*. It is, before caution mitigates it with its domesticating power, absolute and absolutistic. What is stated in it exists thanks to this strength and not because it is true. Creativity is the ability to assert.

Wisdom of the Unfinished

Why should I live in such a way that it makes sense to die?

That death gets all is not a good reason to make a necessity out of it.

I prefer fireworks to the life's work.

Verachtet mir die Meister . . . [1]

Don Alfonso's "Finem Lauda" in *Così fan tutte* should be translated as "Just wait . . . you'll see soon enough that you have nothing to wait for."

Praise the day before it gets dark.

Never to have been born is the proverbial wish of those who cannot accept no longer having anything to expect from death.

Completeness leaves you in the lurch. It passes itself off as the whole, and yet you are still there.

There are pictures that take refuge in the frame, pictures that burst it open and pictures that don't care about it . . .

No source can be answered for.

Having no time—a way to live with the unfinished without having to deal with it.

---

[1] Richard Wagner, *Die Meistersinger von Nürnberg,* act 3, Hans Sachs to Walther: "Verachtet mir die Meister nicht" [Scorn not the masters, I bid you]. *Trans.*

For the incomplete person who believes that something can still become of him, the office he holds is his self-worth. If he no longer believes in this, he believes either that he is fully adequate for the office, or it satisfies him to the full, or he no longer believes in the worth of the office.

If you understand the other you have never encountered him.

The unforeseen is nothing for cautious people.

An improvisation is always provisional.

Fear

The fragment that has been understood is not a fragment anymore. By being ordered into a context it is done away with. Here the process of understanding is a struggle against its object. This shows that an experience of the fragmentary is already at work in the will to understand—in the urge to do away with the fragmentary. This experience precedes the process of understanding and is what starts it in the first place. It is the experience of the impossibility of reducing the fragment to the whole, mastering it. Being deprived of all power does not easily go without fear. The understanding of the fragment that makes the fragment harmless can be understood by way of our fear of the unmasterable.

Order is reassuring. Where it is tidy, I feel safe, at least until something comes to disrupt the order. That order is susceptible to disruptions is a reminder of how precarious it is, and of the fact that one can only ever forget for a short time that it does not include everything. The disruption endangers order. It is experienced as a danger to the extent that order is seen as a value that is hard to give up. Wholeness, coherence, unity, completeness, completion are seldom neutral terms: they are used as value judgments. What is ordered and made into a whole is regarded as meaningful, what is meaningful as valuable. Understanding, as production of coherence, is doubtlessly regarded as meaningful. That order is valuable may go without saying for the understanding, which creates it in the first place; the understanding, however, cannot give its own activity meaning, since it is not by it that values are set. Understanding as determination of meaning is not already meaningful in itself as process, but only from the moment that order is held to be a desirable goal. This happens because what can be brought into a structure of meaning can be made use of and mastered and thus stops being disquieting. Understanding as ordering is a struggle

40

against the threat of the unmasterable, order the answer to our fear of it. It is fear that posits order as a value, because to understand is to subjugate and what is understood is no longer threatening. Thus one can see the reductive understanding of the fragment, its integration into the order of whole and parts, as an attempt to explain away what endangers the safety of the order.

This explanation of the will to understand, like all similar ones, suffers from the fact that it is affected by its own argument. Not only does it, too, serve to bring its object under control, but it, too, must be subjected to its own critique and examined with respect to the role fear plays in it. The understanding of the will to understand as due to fear cannot be an exception to itself. Otherwise it is in its turn a reductive understanding. Once the fear of the unmasterable is identified as what underlies the will to understand, the process of understanding can no longer ignore this, but must recognize that fear has an influence on it as well. Precisely the denial of this influence is what prevents the unmasterable from being approached by the understanding.

The will to understand is provoked by fear. To understand is to attempt to achieve control of what one has not mastered by integrating it into a system of meaning. But the fear of the unmasterable, the driving force of this process, is itself unmasterable. Fear, the defense against the unmasterable, at the same time leaves one defenseless against it. In the resistance against the unmasterable, the unmasterable itself is master. To understand may be to order and to order, to master, but the positing of order as a value on the part of the fear of the unmasterable is beyond the reach of order and mastery. The will to understand, which strives for order, is not reasonable and does not rest on decisions that are justified by rational arguments. I have no choice between wanting and not wanting order. Fear constrains me.

The urge to understand is irrational and uncontrollable. Understanding, I constantly work on overcoming the unmasterable, which manifests itself in the will to understand.

The insight into the role the unmasterable itself plays in the struggle against it restricts the sway of order: order cannot be taken entirely seriously anymore, since it can no longer be expected to disarm that against which it is established. No order can get over what it puts in order, because what escapes it is also at work in it. In the face of this contradiction, the process of understanding must finally forfeit its claim to mastery. The understanding that is achieved by the discovery that fear is at the basis of the process of understanding no longer gives any power over what has been understood, and therefore also fails to free from fear; instead it destroys the illusion that to understand is to conquer through order. No order can ever be done with what is ordered in it. Thus every order makes ever new attempts necessary or possible and always has a certain sense of arbitrariness about it. Every order that has to acknowledge something that is not subjected to it remains a provisional fiction. When it is recognized as such it loses its value, which is neutralized by the fact that the claim to mastery through order is dropped. When wholeness is no longer held in such high regard, the not-whole becomes accessible. In it the unmasterable, whose existence had been denied by order's claim to mastery, becomes perceptible. Fragmentariness cannot be overcome. If an understanding of the fragment is possible, it cannot be an understanding that, ordering, masters, but only one that sees through the arbitrariness of the contexts it puts together and that opens them over and over again to the unmasterable, which only reaffirms itself in them. Such an understanding renounces closure and wholeness because it is only in this way that what is to be understood can remain reachable in its unreachability; such an understanding is in its essence— or in the trouble of its inessence—fragmentary. It grasps and leaves meaning at the very edge of meaning, where meaning no longer is yet where one cannot do without it; where the impossibility of meaning does not let the quest for it break off, because the fear of meaninglessness drives it on: at the breaking point of the fragment.

Superfluousness

(1) The Superfluous

What is in excess is left over. That for which there is no more room within the limits of the whole is what exceeds the whole and is therefore superfluous. Since it does no damage to the order of the whole, it seems negligible. But only from the point of view of a finite whole is it possible to overlook and pass over the superfluous. The infinite whole, outside of which there is nothing, does not admit anything superfluous. What is in surplus with regard to a particular order proves to be again a useful part in a more comprehensive order. When the pitcher overflows, this means only that it is full. From the point of view of the capacity of the pitcher, one can regard the excess water as superfluous and shake it off, but one can also replace the pitcher with a larger one that can hold it all. Strictly speaking, only what cannot be accommodated in any order is superfluous, or, to say it differently, there is superfluousness only when all order is finite. The assumption of the infinite whole as order excludes the possibility that something may not be put in a meaningful relation with something else and therefore integrated. As soon as something—no matter how little—is superfluous, no order is the whole and the whole is no order, because then there still is something outside of every order. As soon as something is not included in any order, everything is superfluous, even order itself, because what cannot be fit into it is not affected by it and has as little use for order as it is of use to it. For that which has escaped all order, order becomes useless.

What is in excess is, seen from the perspective of order, what ought not to exist: the scandal, that with which one does not know what to do and which one cannot be done with. Orderly people try to forget it or point to the future: it only looks as though something were superfluous; later, as soon as we have a large enough pitcher, it will be possible to integrate and understand it. But either there is no superfluousness, or what is superfluous remains forever impossible to integrate. However, the fact that the superfluous cannot be arranged into an order does not mean that it is hostile to order. It appears as the denial of order only to those who are committed to order out of fear. The superfluous is not disorder. One can confront disorder by putting it in order. Order and disorder still belong, as clean opposition, in the order of affirmation and negation. The superfluous, however, is no longer related to order in such a way that it can still be absorbed by it. It refuses antithesis, is not against order and also not simply outside of it: it is outside the opposition of order and disorder. The superfluous does no damage to the ordered whole: it simply lets it be, it neutralizes it. It is not in contrast to the whole, but is no longer relevant for the whole and the whole is no longer relevant for it. The superfluous does not belong, but its not-belonging is without negativity. Since it fits neither the order nor the opposition to it, the superfluous does not just frustrate the attempt to subject it to order: it is not even exposed to it.

From the standpoint of order, the superfluous, which is inaccessible to order, is a scandal. The claim to power that is at work in all ordering does not admit that something may irrevocably elude it. The reverse, however, is not true: the superfluous has no standpoint and no will to mastery; it is beyond antithesis and neither wants to exert mastery nor lets itself be mastered. What is superfluous exerts mastery without being concerned with power. It exerts mastery as superfluousness outside the records, and its lack of concern is its sovereignty.

(2) Wealth

Superfluousness is the excess that is experienced as wealth. It is not he who has enough who is wealthy, but he who has more than enough. Luxury is superfluous and is an indication that someone is outside of the order. It is the unproductive overspending of the excess, a disruption of the balance of giving and taking, which can be afforded only by those who have more than they need. The wealthy person, however, is unproductive only insofar as luxury is not useful under the terms of the order of ends and means, that is, insofar as it does not serve a purpose and therefore eludes this order. But when serving a purpose becomes questionable as a value, it might be that luxury is the only product that carries with it the admission of its origin in superfluousness, because it does not pretend to be useful. For nothing originates where there is no excess. God is a name for superfluousness. The resources he draws from may be unlimited, but he is still outside their limit. Every production, considered as dissipation of surplus energy, is luxury. All order has its condition of possibility in superfluousness, and cannot include it in itself. By denying superfluousness, making light of it as superfluous or condemning it as luxury, order closes itself up to its own condition of possibility. It, too, exists only thanks to excess and is, from the perspective of indifferent generative power, merely discharge of excess. When the superfluous orders itself, a world is created— but only at the expense of the memory of that world's origin. This origin becomes present again only when one stops worrying about order and lets the excess inaccessible to it overflow. When the feeling for excess as condition of possibility expresses itself—in the stammering of happiness, in the exuberance of the lover—discourse easily becomes fragmentary. It breaks off before the break-in of that which it cannot include; its order does not match up to the excess and is thrown off balance by it.

(3) The Unbearable

What surpasses the measure of the bearable is too much and becomes unbearable. Unbearableness is the threat constituted by something superfluous that cannot be dismissed and ignored: one is unable to get over the disturbance it causes but also to shoulder it. What is too much and becomes impossible to bear reveals weakness without helping to counter it. The unbearable is an unfulfillable demand that cannot be disregarded. But unbearableness is not a moral problem. Not being able to cope with the unbearable does not make one guilty: it is simply the experience of unbearableness. By exposing me to an excess with which I am unable to deal in any way, the unbearable tears me away from the protection of the outermost order I am capable of. When I experience the unbearable I am—if "I" means what is within the reach of the ordering subject—outside of myself, at the point where "I" have nothing more to say. And yet I am still there. It is true that I no longer have a stand and cannot take one either, and the possibility of deciding on my conduct is taken away from me, but I still exist as the one who bears the unbearable as that which cannot be borne. In fact, the unbearable does not overwhelm. It is not the burden that crushes that is unbearable. One does not break down under an unbearable burden. There is nothing unbearable about the breakdown, because in it the experience of unbearableness is not tolerated anymore. One experiences the intolerable only so long as one tolerates it. In this untenable tolerating, the moment in which one cannot go on any more extends into something with a duration. Tolerating, I stubbornly remain at the breaking point of the fragment—at my own breaking point, expropriated from me, where the excess does not stop unbearably befalling me.

Readability of the Fragment

It is not certain that talking about fragmentariness brings one closer to it. The depiction of several fragmentary states is perhaps a better approach than the attempt to define the fragment as an object, but then only if one does not avoid the question of the relationship of such states to the reading of fragmentary texts. This relationship would be misunderstood if one wanted to construe it as a psychological explanation of the fragment, as though one spoke fragmentarily when one is sad, embarrassed, or indifferent. Although this may be the case, the attempt to find a causal connection between a state of mind and a way of speaking would cover up once again what should be uncovered. The states described here are not something that would underlie the one or the other fragmentary text, something to which it could therefore be traced back; they are everyday experiences that are akin to those made by whoever sees himself exposed to the fragment. Common to them all is the refusal to fit into an order, which means that the possibility of choosing a behavior [sich verhalten] is taken away. All order is relation [Verhältnis] and guarantees a reference point. Outside the order there are no more opposites, and I, too, am not anymore once nothing else defines me. Falling out of the relation [Verhältnis] is a kind of death that is survived. The anonymous, posthumous endlessness of the person who waits or who is sad is also the condition provoked by the fragment. The fragment is the text that one falls out of.

The fragment is unreadable: it has not been read when one takes notice of what is there nor can one read more than what is there. The fragment is fragmentary because it says less than it should. Something is not there, and this lack must be read as well. This is why it is not possible to talk about the fragment without also talking about what is not there. In the face of the fragment a basic methodological rule for rigor in speaking about texts fails: the rule that what is said must be corroborated by the text, must stand its test. The fragmentary nature of the fragment can only ever be experienced by getting beyond its breaking point, where it has stopped and one is left behind without the expectation of an end having been fulfilled. This fragmentary experience, as an experience of fragmentariness, is not negative but neutral. In it the lack is not negation of fullness (that would still maintain the fixed reference point of the polarity and thereby the possibility of order and of completing the fragment): the lack is here opaque emptiness without opening, without extension or end, without a view on an opposite: exterior.

This experience belongs to the reading of the fragmentary text if the text is read as such, that is, in its breaking off, and if this is still reading. I read the text, but how do I read its stopping short? This event is not told, it just happens—incomprehensibly. In the breaking off, which is not an end but unmotivated stopping, what matters is not what is there in the form of a text. The text breaks off precisely to the extent that its stopping cannot be explained through what is there. Nevertheless the moment when the fragmentary text breaks off also belongs to one's experience of it, an experience that does not stop at the breaking point but outlasts it. Fragmentary states are ways of experiencing the condition provoked by the breaking off of the fragment.

Nothing of these states survives in the—also possible—mere description of the fragment's incompleteness. The fragmentary text is the text from which something is missing. That something is missing from it can only be seen from what is there. Incompleteness is perceived because not every element of the text that one has can be related to something else in a satisfactory manner. The unfinished text contains elements that do not signify, that do not fulfill their referential function because of the missing context. The reference that does not arrive anywhere keeps unfulfilled expectation in suspense. The text from which something is missing does not supply what would be required to understand it. So long as something remains unrelated, there is too little there. But one can say just as well, inversely, that the fragmentary text contains too much. The elements in it that cannot be related to anything and therefore are not meaningful are superfluous. It is this superfluous quantity that makes it impossible to conceive the text as a whole. So the deficiency in meaning is at the same time, if one looks at it differently, an excess of signs. But this observation provides no access to fragmentariness: it merely names it from the standpoint of order. In contrast, the unconcerned person experiences excess and the one who waits, deficiency. Such states are answers to the incomprehensibility of the fragmentary.

FRAGMENTARY
STATES

Living Fragmentarily

To live as though no end were in store, or as though everything were already over. To do without the end. Being mortal is convenient. Who has death before him always has something to plan for. The end makes life into a task. One lives one's life in view of the end, makes it into a destination from which the path will, retrospectively, have been meaningful. If one is prepared to recognize it as necessary, death produces the illusion that life is a whole. But why should death be the end rather than merely the interruption of life? Only because I make it into an end by subjecting what I do not understand to a law of causality I have myself made up. To live life in view of death serves only to justify the ruse that makes death into the goal of life in order to justify living life in view of death. But one needs the end only if one wants completion. When wholeness falls apart as a value, no foreseeing or overview of life is possible. Life can stop, no matter what course it takes, at any time or never. Death is a break, not an end.

The life that can no longer be understood from the end becomes discontinuous and makes biography impossible. Once the expectation of the end disappears, planning, as orientation towards the future, is dropped too. Actions lose their purposiveness, become incomprehensible and drift loosely about. One lives the gap as the impossibility and needlessness of connection, tolerates the final character of unfinishedness. Unfinishedness is not only the possibility of completion. Completion is also the disavowal of what opens up in unfinishedness, pointing beyond its deficiency understood as mere lack of wholeness. In unfinishedness the possibility of completion is at the very least put into question. However, when something that is unfinished can no longer be completed, it is also no longer unfinished, since the decision that something is unfinished is only possible from the point of view of what is finished. What cannot be completed—what is fragmentary—is neither unfinished nor finished.

This neither/nor living is called living fragmentarily.

This neither . . . nor living is called living fragmentarily.

This neither nor living is called living fragmentarily.

Fragmentariness offers no morals. To live fragmentarily means to live without indications about how one should live. Fragmentariness excludes prescription. The only possible answer to the question "How does one live fragmentarily?" is that one cannot. One lives fragmentarily when one cannot go on any more, when one has nothing to expect from the future except that one has none. One lives posthumously and above all without asking how one lives. He who is concerned about that worries about future, goal, and purpose, and has something to live for. Everybody has this. But not everybody loses it, and of those who lose it most find it again. He who does not find it lives fragmentarily, in a closeness to the present with which no meaning interferes, inconsiderately and imprudently. He neither shapes nor destroys. To him order is no more good than disorder is evil. He does not oppose the one to the other: he eludes the order of the opposition. To live fragmentarily is not to live in a disorderly fashion, but to live without faith in the stability of order. The feeling of the arbitrariness and, finally, of the futility of all orders cannot be accommodated in any order: it throws one out of every order. This feeling is the sovereignty of the one who is powerless: he breaks off when he cannot stop, and goes on when he is finished.

In the face of fragmentariness responsibility fails, since it is tied to the possibility of events following each other in a causally determined and consequential way. Responsibility is the pleasure of the orderly person. The person who takes responsibility looks ahead and behind. He stands by the consequences of his actions and never washes his hands of anything he has done. Responsibility presupposes the continuity and unity of the person. When this continuity and unity disintegrates and the breaks, interruptions, and cracks can no longer be covered over, responsibility crumbles away, too.

Living fragmentarily is inconsistent and irresponsible . . . living.

One cannot make a moral system out of this. As soon as an exhortation to live irresponsibly is made—one should no longer take responsibility—responsibility is again brought up. But to live irresponsibly does not mean to live according to a system of non- or antimorals that would decline responsibility: it means living without responsibility. The irresponsible person does not fight responsibility—it has escaped him. He does not live against it but without it. It is of no concern to him and he does not talk about it: he is simply outside of it—and outside himself, too, if "self" means only that in a person for which one can take responsibility. One lives fragmentarily, but one cannot conduct oneself fragmentarily. There are no rules of conduct for this life. Wanting to profess it makes it impossible. Fragmentariness is not a way of life one chooses in the same way as one moves to the country. One lives fragmentarily when one has forgotten the whole, not when one decides to do without it.

Fragmentariness offers no morals. But precisely this can be its moral significance. Because it cannot be grasped morally, it puts a limit to all morals. To live fragmentarily as living fragmentariness is to live without morals. Fragmentary states, which are not accessible from the point of view of the whole, are extramoral. In them life appears detached from all the orders of value that guide one's conduct. The fact that there are situations in which morals are no longer what matters limits their claim to validity. Fragmentariness offers no morals; however, it does offer a critique of morals. The experience of fragmentariness shows each order to be arbitrary: in the face of this arbitrariness each order can be valid only provisionally and is always replaceable. Moral systems that lay claim to definitive validity are bad. In order to be acceptable, they must be accompanied by the awareness that they are arbitrary and therefore insufficient. This insight can never ground a moral stance for those who live fragmentarily and remain without morals just as before; instead, it is the possibility for the moralist to take fragmentariness seriously and still be able to remain moral. This is the only demand that the fragmentary can make of moral systems: that they not try to take responsibility for more than can be taken responsibility for. Of course the claim to validity is necessary to the law. But to posit [setzen] a law [Gesetz] as definitive is usurpation. No human law—and we do not have another one—can overcome its status as linguistic position [Setzung] and the lack of a guarantee. Every order is a fiction, and the awareness that it is linguistic is what makes it provisional. All definitiveness is only violent assertion; fragmentariness, in its being outside the law, is the unmasking of this assertion. What is most definitive about morals is that they are provisional. When someone comes back into an order from the irresponsibility of discontinuous life, this fact does not disappear.*

---

* The irresponsible person of whom I speak here is not far from the one who is not legally responsible for his actions. Legal irresponsibility is the disruption of the continuity of the person. It is a great accomplishment of the law to admit that there are aspects of humanity that order cannot reach, and that actions which are, in their effects, disruptive of order can bring into view things that do not fall under the jurisdiction of order. However, the matter does not rest there: jurisdiction is immediately turned over to another order. What cannot be classified as good or evil is referred to the health-illness scale of values. Cure replaces punishment.

Waiting

Mostly, waiting is expectation. One waits for something, which one supposes, fears or hopes will happen. When someone waits for something, he is entirely fulfilled by what he expects. He looks forward to it so much that he hardly allows himself really to experience the wait. Waiting is something that one has to put up with for the sake of a purpose, something entirely temporary, mere condition of fulfillment, a state of lack that one wants to overcome as fast as possible. One stops waiting as soon as one gets what one wants. The possession puts out the expectation. To understand waiting as expectation is to think it from the point of view of totality. One who waits is in a state of incompleteness and waits for completion. Expectation always aims at remedying a lack. It is the experience of a momentary imbalance in the budget of the whole. When the expectation is fulfilled order is reestablished.

Yet there is a waiting without expectation. It can set in when one has waited for something so long, without seeing any signs of imminent fulfillment, that the object of expectation gradually begins to fade, and yet one does not stop waiting. The state of unfulfillment lasts unchanged, but the hope of putting an end to it has been imperceptibly eroded and the waiting has become empty, mere opening onto infinite lack. But the fulfillment, too, brings nothing different. When someone has everything, he has nothing more to expect. Nonetheless he waits, although there no longer is an object of expectation. He who has fullness goes over into the superfluous. The waiting of the one who has everything is superfluous waiting. But it is, as superfluous, at the same time unavoidable, since there still is a future that one cannot not wait for, even when one has nothing to expect from it. Expecting as waiting for fullness is resolved in fulfillment. But there remains a waiting beyond fulfillment, for which fulfillment and completion are not enough anymore, a waiting no longer for the whole but outside of it, where there is nothing more that is still missing and could be waited for.

While all expectation plans for the future and is directed to a purpose, there is no distracting justification that could be used as protection against the experience of pure waiting. Pure waiting takes place when the whole is no longer expected, either because it has been forgotten or because it is complete, although it is not the case that "everything is finished." When the future has nothing more to promise that is not there already, expectation becomes waiting. Waiting cannot be fulfilled. In it lasts a present that breaks off, does not stop breaking off, because no future moment is able to develop and change the present one. Every *now*, a breaking point inaccessible to completion, rises up into emptiness. This duration of the break is the experience of fragmentariness in waiting. The fragment does not belong to expectation, because it does not expect to be completed. The fragment is waiting. What makes the fragment fragmentary is the fact that its incompletion does not create any expectation, but starts one waiting, far from any object of expectation.

Boredom

It gets boring when time is empty, when one does not need it, when there is nothing to do. It is not that a bored person would not have work to do, but that it is not worth the trouble for him—in fact, not even the trouble is worth the trouble. Before he begins he already has everything behind and nothing ahead of him. He has always already anticipated whatever he could decide to take up. Why make plans, when everything is leveled out already?

But empty time weighs on one because it becomes boring. It is not what happens that is heavy, but the fact that nothing happens that would help pass the time [was die Zeit vertreibt]. In the pastime-greenhouse [Zeitvertreibhaus] time puts forth [treibt] colorless, fruit-less blossoms, grows up high into a monstrous ulcer of nothingness, and those who are bored pay admission in order to see that nothing is as imperishable as time. The number one draws at the entrance for the aim-, purpose-, meaning- or time(less) lottery [das Ziellos, Zweck-los, Sinnlos oder Zeitlos] is never the winning one. Afterwards it has gotten a little later.

While all is fulfilled, time empties itself out. Boredom is almost hap-piness. Time is what is too much for those who lack nothing. To have everything and then time on top of it is the boredom of the happy person. In it he would tolerate the time if time were not unbear-able.

The bored person cannot endure boredom, yet has nothing with which to oppose it. He would not like something else instead of it. How could he, without interest? He cannot approve of his state: in order to do so he would have to take an interest in it. Maybe he would like to want it all to stop: not this instead of that, but nothing instead of all—boredom waits for death, said the *Rheinischer Hausfreund*.[1] But when one has everything and experiences nothing except that it all goes on nonetheless, boredom is precisely the experience of its own not stopping. In it the end is already over and, since it has not been the end, it is also unmasked as the illusion of the interested person. Only, there is no point in knowing this, since it is only now that it all begins not to end.

---

[1] *Schatzkästlein des rheinischen Hausfreundes* (1811), a collection of tales by Johann Peter Hebel. *Trans.*

Slowness

There is the slowness of deliberation, of the person who is too cir-cumspect to rush things. It is not without self-complacency and appears together with the embonpoint of the contented person who thinks he is master of the situation. But there is also a slowness that has nothing to do with planning or with overview, but only with the almost too great difficulty of every moment. A person who is slow in this sense simply cannot go any faster. He is not lazy, and never could be. He always needs everything he has, and it is never enough.

Perhaps slowness has no limits, but there is a limit to how much the operations it affects can be slowed down. When an activity does not run its course at a certain speed—one not too close to immobility—it falls apart. Its purposefulness is lost. And when the action's purpose fades, its meaning does too. The movements of the slow person lack the sober purposiveness that the fast one has as a matter of course because he never has to think about it. The slow person never makes it to the point where he can pursue an end. What is only a means to an end for the fast person is for him an almost unreachable goal. This is why everything he does appears detached from the purpose that it could actually serve, and gives the impression of being erratic, disconnected, monstrously an end in itself. And yet this expresses nothing but his inability to master the means.

The slow person is never done. Because he knows no end, he also cannot set priorities or practice foresight. He always has before him an obstacle that cannot be overcome: the fact that something should be done right now for which there is no time. He agrees on this with the hasty and the rushed. With the difference that the reason why he has too little time is not that he has too much to do, but that he is too slow. All his plans crumble away as they are carried out. So he is without a goal. In a world suited to him it would not matter whether or not one is done.

Indifference and Unconcernedness

The indifferent person lives in freedom from values. He does not prefer anything because things do not have different worth to him. Whether he does one thing or another is just as much without consequence as whether he does anything at all. Should he resolve on an activity, it also does not matter where he starts and stops, since he could just as well have done neither. All his decisions are random and each could also turn out the opposite way. To him, all differences are leveled out. Everything is bathed in the same gray light that makes everything look the same. Values disintegrate for him because the order in whose framework they are valid appears to him, as a whole, random. His view has turned so much into overview that all things become equivalent to him, paling in their individuality and losing their value. He sees everything at the same time and therefore cannot remain inside anything. He is too far away to be able to gain a foothold on anything. His world is monotonous. His movements are not purposeful and the path that he follows is without aim, because he proceeds on it with the feeling that every other path would be neither better nor worse: merely to pass the time. The indifferent person never brings anything to an end because for him there is no end. He is always just as far whether he is here or there. Thus he can break off at any time, but also go on at any time. He is never at his destination and yet always already as far as he can go. Where he pauses, everything is lacking, and nothing changes about it when he goes on. He is fragmentary not only because he breaks off, but also because he cannot stop. He might stop somewhere because there is no point in continuing, but since there is also no point in stopping, he might not do that either. Abruptness and endlessness are indifferent to him. The break is the incapacity to end.

The unconcerned person has no overview. For him there is only what comes immediately next and the instant. In this way he seems to privilege the only thing that really matters, but he, too, has no value system. He does not make a decision to exclude the other things, the things he is not concerned about: he simply does not see them. He is blind to all that is no cause of concern for him, and thus also to what he does. What is of no concern for him is the context and the question of meaning. While the indifferent person is unable to remain within the context because he overlooks it from afar and sees through its fragility, the unconcerned person is outside order because it has not at all become a cause of concern for him yet. He gives himself over to the overplenty of the moment far too much for there to be anything else for him. The unconcerned person is vital. He lives out of the surplus of the moment without asking what purpose what he does could serve. One has no use for him, and when one abuses him he is not affected by it so long as he remains unconcerned. He is extraordinary in his bubbling naïveté, whose creations always seem somewhat bizarre to the cool look of the orderly person. He brings nothing to a conclusion, not because he finds that it isn't worth it, but because of the excess [*Übermass*] of things he has surging up from inside him that keep him forever at the source and hinder his patiently giving shape to anything, but also his experiencing this as a hindrance. The unconcerned person does not measure [*misst*], because he has no sense of measure [*Mass*]. What is at work in the unconcerned is excess [*Übermass*]. If nothing comes to a conclusion, it is because something new always already presents itself before the old project has had a chance to be developed. The unconcerned person knows no continuity other than that of the things that occur to him, tripping over themselves. He never asks himself what they are worth and what could be made of them, but creates without reflection, so that he never has the product before his eyes but is always just lightly squandering the surplus he has.

The unconcerned person is indifferent towards his creations, but his indifference is an unknowing one. The indifferent person is not concerned with anything because he sees too much; the unconcerned person is indifferent because he sees too little. The vitality of the one is blind, the clear-sightedness of the other is sterile. The one cannot come all the way up to the order that the other has already behind him. The unconcerned person is preparatory just as the indifferent one is posterior. Since there is no system of values in which the unconcerned person could be bound, he is perhaps the happy one, and the unhappiness of the indifferent person is the experience of the impossibility to still perceive as a fault his inability to prefer one thing to another.

The indifferent and the unconcerned person belong together: as not belonging. But the order that is formed by this belonging together cannot penetrate the states of unconcernedness and indifference, which, as ways of not belonging, always remain outside of the relation into which they are brought. The unconcerned and the indifferent person come to no understanding, so very close and yet so very foreign they are to each other. The unconcerned person knows nothing of the indifferent one, who in turn does not care about him. And yet where people talk in such a way—fragmentarily, that is—that no work comes about, both of them are always at work. Without the unconcerned person talking would not begin, and without the indifferent person it would not break off or go on endlessly. The unconcernedness with which the superfluous pours itself out is just as incomprehensible as the indifference in which it affirms itself as superfluous. Without encountering each other meaningfully in a common sphere, the unconcerned and the indifferent person dwell outside the matter-of-factness with which the concerned, interested person makes himself useful between beginning and end and tries to draw satisfaction from the round fruits of his work.

Exhaustion

One who is exhausted cannot go any further and remains lying on the way. He comes up to the limit of possibility, but not to his destination. His lack of strength deprives him of power. The strong person is the active one, the one who gets his own way and puts his strength in the service of a cause. He performs tasks and gets his job done. All this is lost in the fatigue of the exhausted person, who lives without having a hold on himself. Since he cannot go on anymore, he must do without power. He survives the possibility of making it in life. The person who lets himself go after reaching his destination is only tired. The exhausted person is never where he would like to be. He did not have enough strength. He is never finished.

He has taken on too much, or too much has been demanded of him. His performance does not correspond to the expectations. Exhaustion disrupts an economy in which the goal is measured by strength and in which effort and performance are values. This order can disintegrate when one cannot go on anymore. In exhaustion, effort still appears only as the failed attempt to cover up its own futility, and performance only as the cramped-up denying of the limit of what one can do, the limit at which the unmasterable befalls the exhausted person. That strength runs out does not mean that a little more would have sufficed, but that the realm of possibility has been exhausted. Exhaustion is the experience of the impossible in which failure disappears. The exhausted person has not just been too weak: he escapes the order of energy and performance and falls into the impossibility of performance, where performance is no longer valid or its value becomes indifferent.

The exhausted person must live without the order, since he did not measure up to it. He has no place in it anymore; precisely for this reason, however, he has also grown beyond and out of it and sees the limit of performance. Whether someone is exhausted sooner rather than later does not change anything in the fact that at some point one cannot go any further, although one has not yet arrived. When it comes to this point one breaks off and lives on with the impossibility of going on. This cannot be endured unless one regains one's strength. But the strengthened person, who endures exhaustion, does not again subordinate the strength he has recovered, as means, to the goal that escaped him when he was exhausted. He lives fragmentarily. Strength goes up in smoke. There is no point in strength. It is nothing but the superfluous exhausting itself.

Improvisation

It happens that a crisis forces one to improvise. The crisis is the un-foreseen, that which one never encounters otherwise than unprepared. The improviser has the ability to make the best out of a difficult situation with what is at hand right then. Provoked by the challenge of the moment, he suddenly recognizes possibilities never dreamed of before and is able to replace what is not there with what is. He is an unparalleled maker of metaphors and can build in no time a replace-ment world in place of the order that the unexpected, breaking in, has destroyed—a world that works, although, being an emergency solution, it openly shows its incompleteness and remains provisional with respect to the order that it stands for.

But why improvise only when one must? Since no order is definitive, each order only stands for another that is not there. Whoever takes any order seriously wakes up when it breaks down in the face of the unexpected and he has to hold himself above water by improvising. The memory of such times spent on the limit of the possible survives long after the semblance of regulated life has regained predominance and marks it as semblance by keeping alive what derides all planning. No precaution can prevent the occurrence of the unforeseen. Prepar-ing oneself for it one lives improvisationally, in hourly expectation of the unexpected. Then, one has more foresight than those who believe in their own constructions, since one recognizes from the beginning as provisional what the planner considers definitive until he fails. The improviser takes the precaution of taking no precautions. He lives from day to day, as well as he can. And he can do a great deal. Out of little he makes much and in most cases does just the right thing for that moment. He has the lightness and superiority of the tightrope-walker and also his elegance. With every step he saves his balance. But he never embarks on more than is necessary just then. He has no great plans for his life and no goals except to make it further, as well as it goes. He is inconsistent and should not be taken at his word. Little matters to him.

There is the improvisation of the unconcerned person who, at any moment and without a goal, arranges what is lying around, as one does with flowers, into a bunch of meanings. But improvisation is also a possible way of life for the one who has come back from the point where he could not go any further. Big constructions are not worth it for him. He detaches himself from them before he undertakes them. His breaking off [Abbrechen] is already implicit when he begins, and it undermines every project. To improvise: to begin somehow and see what comes out. To begin [anbrechen], to set out [aufbrechen] instead of breaking off [abbrechen]. The improviser does not live outside the order but with the awareness of its arbitrariness. Like the planner, he too orders, but always provisionally and sometimes playfully: throwing constellations like dice.

Daredevil

The daredevil, who goes for it all, is a fragmentarist. Because he is thought of as powerful, it is too readily assumed that he is master of the situation, while on the contrary he gives himself over to it in full possession of his powers. However determined he is to win, he nonetheless never knows how it will all turn out. The unpredictability of the outcome is inseparable from his daredevilry. The daredevil needs luck, and when he has it he fascinates—an almost mythical figure—because it looks as though he stood under supernatural protection. Uncontrollable factors are invariably instrumental in his successes. But his attitude is not that of the believer who confides in God's help: at most he confides in himself and as for the rest he dives into the risk. He does not live on the belief in a global order but on the excitement of the unforeseen. He loves uncertainty, it lures him, and he acts not, like the goal-driven, cautious person, to get rid of it, but to play around in it like the swimmer who is always diving into the next wave. He is an adventurer: something unexpected is always in store for him. The life situations in which he appears do not afford a clear view of themselves: they can only be solved by staking everything on one card. In these cases, the merit of winning is limited since luck was involved, and losing is not a failure, since one has done what one could. The daredevil is neither right nor wrong. He cannot be justified, but cannot be condemned either. Neither does he act reasonably nor could one, were one in his situation, do better or, much less, prepare in advance. His decisions are a gambler's bets. He lives on the edge of life, where every step is a venture; he does not settle anywhere and nothing holds him back. But his unbridledness is not that of someone who has lost control: he remains sober even in the inebriation of danger. He is guided by no conviction, succumbs to no passion. Deep inside him extends flat and endless the wasteland beyond the last settlement. It is because he has it inside him that he is a daredevil. By the leap with which he breaks away every time from the realm of responsible actions he only takes into himself the outside into which he has always already slipped away. The self-control that distinguishes him is preserved only because he perpetually lets himself go in order to get a grip on himself. He knows that perhaps one time or another luck will abandon him and he will have to dare the devil in person. But what could stop him? And from what should he be stopped? The courage of the daredevil is without ambition, almost indifferent. He lives—as one can still live after noticing that one actually cannot—in the impossible. He makes being overtaxed into a profession. For some he becomes a hero because he manages to do more than can reasonably be demanded. But he can only do that because he is no longer concerned by the fact that the demands are ultimately always greater than what one can do. The insight that it is not worth it is what makes him free to act. He goes to the limit because he is beyond it in advance and does not expect anything more from it than to be wholly in unfinishedness, which is the last thing.

Embarrassment

The irony of this discourse is that it is not possible to comment on breaking off. What breaks off justifiably has ended. The discourse that is able to say why it breaks off is not fragmentary. Only that breaks off which, stopping, is no longer in control of itself and does not stop where it actually should. The break does not announce its coming, and afterward it is too late to say anything more. Breaking off is the mute crossing into wordlessness, senseless stopping at the wrong moment. There is nothing to say about it.

Except that there are states in which there is nothing to say. At the breaking point of the fragment talking stops and what should have been said has not been. But it is not only that there is something missing here: the possibility of remedying the lack by talking on is also missing, because what there still would have been to say does not exist. To look for it is futile and to believe one has found it is only to flee from the break-off as the experience that it all goes on although one cannot go on. Although nothing more comes, it is also not over. There is nothing to say and yet one is not at the end. The fragment is talking that is neither finished nor able to go on. It is neither finite, since it has no end, nor infinite, since it stops.

The wish to talk about the experience of the fragmentary puts one in an embarrassing situation *[bringt in Verlegenheit]*. But this means that when one is embarrassed one is close to the fragmentary. One should speak and cannot. The embarrassed person *is* fragment. He breaks off. Not because he does not dare to speak, but because what should be said escapes him, because he misplaces *[verlegt]* and loses it. He has nothing to say and knows only that there would be something to say and that he cannot say it. The embarrassed person has no inner wealth to which he is merely unable to give expression: he dries out where the paralysis of the tongue seizes him and he stutters himself away. There is nothing to expect from him; he does not have the depth of still waters. His failure is without reason, deep or otherwise, his falling silent not the silencing of anything. Embarrassment is flat, an emptiness without depth. Here there is nothing to expect from the lack: it is no longer in contrast with fullness and contains no promise of what is missing in it. The lack is endured without the possibility of naming what is lacking. The paralysis of the embarrassed person is the impossibility of resolving the tension at the breaking point where one can neither stop nor continue. In embarrassment the suspense of the break-off has become lasting.

The embarrassed person is cornered into ceaselessness. His straits are boundless.

Speechlessness

When one becomes speechless, voice gives out. It is not words and meanings that fail one, but sounds. Not the sounds with which the words of the language are put together, but the sounds that come out of me and in which I can come out of myself. Becoming speechless I break off. Not just my talking breaks off, but I, who cannot become myself anymore. Although speechlessness seems to leave everything open, nothing is stored up in it. Nothing is silenced, because there is nothing there. That is why speechlessness is only apparently a leaving open—the reserve from which it would be possible to extract something is not there. The person who becomes speechless has no secret and no unexhausted potentiality that one could make something of. He has no depth at all. The shallowness in which everything lightlessly comes to light, and yet in which everything one would expect is missing, throttles the voice, which has no more space in which to vibrate. Pressed into tonelessness, it dies, because there is nothing inside for it to bring out. Speechlessness has nothing to do with depth. Much rather with running out of breath. Speechlessness *[Verstummen]* is no promise *[Versprechen]*, only a failure *[Versagen]*—not that one could make anything better—a failing of the voice, which some time, when it all becomes too much and one can't do anything, chokes and leaves behind what's too little.

Mourning

One mourns [*trauert*] for what is lost. What is lost has ended. The reason why the end is always sad [*traurig*] is that one survives it since one lives through it. The end is sad because it is only a half end and something else comes after it. What stops in such a way that one loses it while it comes to an end is not completed. If it had been completed it would *be*. What stops without having been completed can no longer become what it would have liked to, could have or should have become. The hope of completion ends with the end. The end of hope survives as mourning. What ends uncompleted breaks off. Where it breaks off, its failure begins. What has failed to happen cannot be made up for. Mourning envelops the emptiness from which nothing more can be expected. One mourns less for what was than for what can no longer happen now. Mourning is a living on without future, in the monotony of the treeless plain in which every place is like the next.

The deepest mourning is flat. The illusion one can lean on that one has lost something one once had is missing from it. The greatest loss is the potentiality of which nothing has come. In the sadness about what never was and now no longer can be, the comfort of at least having had it earlier is missing. This sadness is without homesickness since one was never at home. It prevents any absorption into a past that is becoming blurred in velvet darkness already just by way of the distance, and exposes one to the harsh light of an ineluctable present without potentiality. It befalls the person who is left behind with that of which nothing can come anymore, with what is definitively unfinished, that is, dead. Nothing can be made good in this mourning. The fragment remains unredeemed, spellbound in mere senseless interruption, the fixed photograph of a process that has not taken place. The sadness of the endless moment is the feeling of being in the middle of it and yet at the end, that everything is over except the feeling that it is over.

This is the sadness of the novel, whose story can never come to completion because its end is always followed by its narration. In the posthumous present of narration everything has already happened, and only the pale suspicion remains that nothing more can happen than the narration of what happened. That the story turns into narration is sad because it shows that it has not found its end and that it must keep ending in the narration, unfulfilled. Nothing that is narrated is free from the accompanying uneasiness about the fact that it is narrated out of the futureless present of a neutral Beyond. The narrator is no other than the surviving of the end that, since it has not been one, bathes the narration in sadness about the fact that no end is in sight anymore.

Testament

In his testament a person speaks as though he were already dead. Or as though he still lived. In his testament he finishes off his life before it has ended, but he also prolongs himself. He wants his will to be still valid when he is no longer there. The wish to make dispositions *[verfügen]* beyond the end is the wish to be in control of the end *[über das Ende verfügen]*. Who makes order in his affairs tries to include the end in this order. But by thinking himself capable of making order, he cannot be done with himself. He remains outside the order that he makes, but that he is not.

There is no last will. Everybody survives it. As long as a person writes down what he wants he is not at the end. Between testament and death is the time that one cannot control *[verfügen]*, that one cannot put in order. Life is always longer than the order into which one brings it. The person writing his last will *[der letztwillig Verfügende]* has the last moment, which would be what matters, precisely not at his disposal *[zur Verfügung]*. He lives on in posthumous disorder. The survival of the last will is the dying man's powerless wait for the end. After he has bequeathed everything, he receives himself as the remainder he does not know what to do with. He is left to himself, not having stopped existing yet—in defiance of his own last will. Precisely the testament, which should have made life meaningful up to the end and beyond, makes it superfluous instead. The attempt to keep at least, testamentarily, a firm grip on the way in which one lets oneself out of one's hands only leaves the memory of the rash "last will," which by anticipating the end takes away all expectation of a last thing.

One's own death is always only nearly it.

Broken-off Relationships

When a relationship is broken off, something in the world becomes opaque. Something will now remain forever unresolved. It lies in life's landscape like a mountain that cannot be climbed or a lake that has to be walked around. It is not that we get rid of each other: only, the relationship is no longer ours and slips away into a foreignness that shuts us out. It is not the relationship that stops when it is broken off, but what is no longer possible to make of it. The fixed picture that each has of the other from now on depicts only the weakness of wanting to explain the break in such a way as to make it into an end.

The allegedly dead relationship could be recounted. Should I make a story out of it? But who recounts is not in the state of having broken off. He has made up his mind for fiction. He has something to say and knows nothing of a talking that does not arrive anywhere, of words that fall out of one's mouth like dice without ever hitting a table which could help score a twelve. As long as they fall, the game is interrupted. Haste waits a long time [Eile wartet mit Weile] for the number that does not come. Where counting stops, there is no recounting, either.

The burden: that nothing can be changed anymore, that the unfinished has frozen and is now definitive.

A shadow that nothing casts.

The broken-off relationship goes on, not like any past thing that one remembers having had, but incessantly breaking off, as continuous crossing into the impossibility of getting over it. It is not a relationship that has ended—it is the relationship that consists in no longer associating with each other. As unalterable, it is inevitable. Almost bodily, but ungraspable, blown out and void, it rises up to become what is in me without me. Not belonging from the beginning, the shred hangs in life.

Hopelessness

Hopelessness *[Hoffnungslosigkeit]* is an unnecessarily used-up word. This is because hope is believed to be indispensable. To be without hope is, then, a misfortune. But if hope is a value, then the corresponding negative value is adequately expressed by the word "despair" *[Verzweiflung]*, and "hopelessness" is freed up to designate what it means in its simplest literal sense: a state that is without hope. Precisely not in the sense, however, that one suffers from its lack and despairs because of it, but in the sense that one is rid *[los]* of it— and of despair too. The hopeless person is neither hopeful nor desperate: he has left the order in which the two are opposed to each other as desirable and feared. Hopelessness is a neutral condition in which hope and despair have become equivalent and in which their opposition, which has been left behind, is no longer relevant.

But this way of reading remains, in spite of everything, not sanctioned by language. Language resists hopelessness. Although the word is built in such a way that it does not contain a value judgment on the condition it describes (except for the fact that hope is mostly valued in advance), it still cannot avoid naming hope, which remains present in it as negated and thus does not completely disappear from consideration. It appears that language is only able to affirm and negate. It always posits *[setzen]* and counters its positing *[entgegensetzen]*: thus it is expression of the order that it grounds, the order in which de-posing *[Entsetzen]* is judged from the start as dreadful *[entsetzlich]*, de-speaking *[Entsprechen]* belittled as correspondence *[Entsprechung]*, and answering *[Antworten]* can never be a de-wording *[Entworten]*. The speaker's fear orders language, which then fulfills his hope for order. Neutral hopelessness has no name because in it the order of oppositions that gives language its character is deprived of validity. Language permits reversing valuations but not neutralizing values. Thus one could, of course, reverse the value judgment that has consolidated into a truism in the current linguistic order and speak of "de-hopement" *[Enthoffnung]*; then hope would appear as a bad thing from which one is freed rather than as a good thing that one loses, but one would still not be rid *[los]* of hope, since such a word, as an attempt to put into question the value assigned to hope, would be again the expression of the hope to be able to say hopelessness and therefore to bring it back into the order of language.

Hopelessness is not what language makes it into. It has no name. It cannot be spoken about. For the hopeless person there is no order outside language, and yet he is where language does not arrive, at a point that cannot be included in any order. Hopelessness is the extralinguistic, the feeling that no order is complete. The hopeless person still talks; not, however, because he hopes to be able to say hopelessness, but because he wishes to be able to. He is driven by the hopeless wish for a language in which speaking would not be ordering: a language not of hope but of wish. Hope is only the instrumentalization of the wish in the service of the possible. The wish is independent of the possibility of fulfillment; it is a pure crossing of borders, a hopeless breakout *[Ausbruch]*, a setting out *[Aufbruch]* into the impossible.

Wishlessness

To imagine a talking beyond the wish. Once imagined it is represented, it becomes something to be attained by talking and therefore something wished for, so that the talking beyond the wish is perhaps only thinkable as the object of a wish. But it is doubtful whether such a talking is to be wished for as I imagine it.

The talking beyond the wish has no task. No will drives it. Nothing has to be said, nothing communicated to anyone. This happens, too, but it is not what matters. Communication happens on the side—or in some cases does not happen: then the sound of the voice fades away, or the text is left there. That is not what matters. But what is also there besides is not what matters, either: not the fact that talk has taken place, which is still there in addition to its willful being directed at something; not the paleness of wishless language, which simply takes place. Without the justification of a meaning. Language as foggy-insipid, where one neither loses nor finds one's way.

The talk beyond the wish is carefree. To be without cares is not to be so happy as to have no more wishes. Happiness is not wishless. Cares give you a hold. There are cares only when something is important. When everything is light enough that nothing really matters anymore, there are no weighty matters that one believes one has to take care of. Beyond the wish one talks irresponsibly. The writer [der Schriftsteller], who thinks of himself as the figurehead of society, takes refuge in responsibility. The person who just writes [der Schreibende] has no obligation. He takes place. He wants nothing from others, and so they want nothing from him. Because there are always enough people who want one to want something from them, it goes quite well without him. But there is a remainder: the talking beyond the wish. Although one does not know what to do with it, it does not stop. Since it is irresponsible it can neither be taken at its word nor refuted. By not offering any resistance it resists all attempts to draw it into conversation, and it has always already refused to fit into any order into which one has tried to fit it. As a remainder, it cannot be answered for. It is disturbing precisely because it does not want to disturb and one can do nothing either for or against it.

To talk about unconcerned talking is a sign that one concerns oneself with it, possibly even that it is a cause for concern. Why should it concern me whether my talking is like the talking I imagine? One is unconcerned when one does not care whether one is unconcerned or not.

Whether or not I wish, when I talk of a talking beyond the wish— that should not matter to me. Talking may be explained to me as talking's curse or as being cursed to talk. It does not affect me. It is not me that it affects. I is nothing but the wishless plea for talking.

Absentmindedness

The absentminded person is not "with it." Wherever he is, he is elsewhere. Whatever he does, something else distracts him. One does not really address the issue when one attributes absentmindedness to professors. When someone is so absorbed in something that he does not pay attention to anything else, he is not absent-minded, but concentrating. What is interpreted as absentmindedness in him is on the contrary his strongly focusing on something quite specific, next to which many other things become unimportant. Real absentmindedness is not a side effect of concentration. Absentmindedness has no center. One is not absentminded when one puts an emphasis on other things, but when one puts no emphasis anywhere. The absentminded person is not at home anywhere and has the ubiquity of the vagabond. Charlie Chaplin is sometimes absent-minded. The absentminded person seems to have a farsightedness that the person who is absorbed by something cannot muster, and derives his insights not from his preoccupation with things but, on the contrary, from his not getting involved in anything. This is no asceticism and also no refusal to take things seriously: it happens, as might be expected, out of absentmindedness. The absentminded person is everywhere and nowhere, nowhere entirely and everywhere a little. In his absentmindedness he isn't anyone anymore and yet shows, in his abstraction, an overview that is denied to the person who concentrates. But what seems to be his sense for the whole does not give access to an order. In order to build a world he would have to prefer one thing to another and make it into a center. The absentminded person puts nothing in order. His wisdom consists in the fact that every time that something might keep hold of him something else occurs to him. Because everything is always present to him and he never stays with something for long, he escapes dogmatism and an orderly life escapes him. His world has the innocence of a preworld in which everything lies around in a disorder still free of purpose, or of a postworld that remains when all attempts to make order have been left behind. This pre- and postworldliness is the absentminded person's remoteness, his non-belonging. What one could call his purity shows up in the fact that no one else can start something without thinking about finishing it in the way he can. Only someone who has everything already behind him and is where one neither starts nor stops can start things in this way. The actions of the absentminded person are innocent. Nothing really matters for him. He disperses himself with the liberality of someone who has been freed. Not that this is an achievement and that there is merit in it. He is just absentminded.

On the Side

Some people make all sorts of arrangements before they begin to write. Only the best room in the house is good enough for a study. The desk—finally the only one of the right size, height, and color—is in such a position with respect to the window that the light falls on it from the desired angle. One person wants it cleared up, the other needs it covered with layers of proof of intellectual activity. The sheet of paper in front of which one sits has the particular English format that is so hard to find. One person writes on it in the early morning with a particularly fine fountain pen and exclusively black ink, the other cannot do without his thick green felt-tip pen and cannot imagine any other time to work than the night—and then, of course, one single light, designed not to tire the eyes, has to be on.

Such preparations have a touching ridiculousness about them. They attest to the great importance one gives to one's productions, to how seriously one takes them, and to how hard one tries to produce the most ideal preconditions for the creation of the unique work one expects from oneself. One is reminded of birth clinics that, as a precaution, are equipped to take everything into account that can be beneficial to a gentle birth. However, it must be said that very few children are also conceived in a hospital. For them to be brought into the world with the assistance of all technical means there must be moments in which one neither has nor needs an oxygen mask. Clinical hygiene is not a suitable atmosphere for that. And perhaps the attention to external details is not a suitable one for mental production.

I imagine a person—perhaps it is the same one—who is disturbed, paralyzed even, by the signs of the importance of what he does. Then he has only one thought, and it is how many thoughts he would need to have for all the preparatory measures to be justified. So he throws everything away and goes to a bar, and then maybe he thinks about something and writes it on the back of his ticket in the tram, or a difficulty he has long thought about in vain is suddenly solved when he has drunk too much and wakes up bleary-eyed and unfit to work. Such successes are in no way the result of another kind of preparation. It is of no use to go to a bar in order to be able to write. Rather, what is important is that what is important should happen on the side, which is precisely what is prevented by one's resolution to let it happen on the side. Only that which, when it happens, is not so important happens on the side. What is important is perhaps most likely to occur just when it is unimportant.

The one who writes on the side is happy when things occur to him and tries to make the most out of them, but without ever taking what he does quite seriously. Everything, he thinks, could be just a little different, and it could probably be done without, too. That this is so, however, becomes a serious problem for him every now and then, and he reflects upon it, straining, until something about it dawns on him—on the side.